Angel in Flames

Angel in Flames
Selected Poems & Translations 1967-2011
James Scully

Published 2011by
Smokestack Books
PO Box 408, Middlesbrough TS5 6WA
e-mail : info@smokestack-books.co.uk
www.smokestack-books.co.uk

Angel in Flames
Selected Poems & Translations 1967-2011
Cover image: Masaccio, *Cacciata dei progenitori dall'Eden*,
Santa Maria del Carmine, Florence
Author photograph: Arlene Scully

Printed by
EPW Print & Design Ltd

ISBN 978-0-9564175-8-9
Smokestack Books gratefully
acknowledges the support of
Arts Council England

LOTTERY FUNDED

Smokestack Books is
represented by Inpress Ltd
www.inpressbooks.co.uk

to Bill & Gloria Broder
&
José Ramón Lerma

Where have the weapons gone, peaceful
productive Italy, you who have no importance in the world?
In this servile tranquillity, which justifies

yesterday's boom, today's bust – from the sublime
to the ridiculous – and in the most perfect solitude,
j'accuse! Not, calm down, the Government or the Latifundia

or the Monopolies – but rather their high priests,
Italy's intellectuals, all of them,
even those who rightly call themselves

my good friends. These must have been the worst
years of their lives: for having accepted
a reality that did not exist. The result

of this conniving, of this embezzling of ideals,
is that the real reality now has no poets.
(I? I am desiccated, obsolete.)

from Pier Paolo Pasolini, *Victory*
translated by Norman MacAfee and Luciano Martineng
(Azul Editions)

Contents

Early Poems, 1967-1994

Later Poems, 2004-2011

Horst Bienek

I don't know Horst Bienek
Horst Bienek surely doesn't know me

is he still alive? someone will know

Herr Bienek was or is a journalist
and a poet

I found his defiant lines
Bienek's defiant, wishful lines
translated, awkwardly,
into a musty Penguin paperback:
we speak loudly, no one understands us,
but we're not surprised—
we are speaking the language
that will be spoken tomorrow

young Bienek studying with Brecht
at the Berliner Ensemble in East Berlin

sentenced to hard labor
25 years commuted to 4
in the Vorkuta mines
of the old Soviet Union

for speaking too loudly
the awkwardly translated language
that will be spoken tomorrow

indeed some already speak it
not loudly, but in an ordinary voice
as though there's nothing to it

a language like a bowl of soup
on a cold rainy day
you eat, without thinking about it
or what it took to make this
stuff that sticks to your bones

Listening to Coltrane

listening to Coltrane, hearing
the original people

who abide us, sometimes
kill us

as always
we are killing them –

he blows through all
the abiding and killing

blows the send-off
we got on leaving the cosmos
the beauty of its harmony
behind us, blows

there is never any end,
there are always new sounds
to imagine,
new feelings to get at

squawking
brass, reeds, battered skin
steel wires *there is*

always the need to keep
purifying
these feelings and sounds

honking out over
        our cosmic exile
the bent strains of the original people
their long shadows riding shotgun on his wing

to give the best of what we are

Liberation of Paris

o liberation of Paris

citizens on the street
happy to see us o
beside themselves
leaping on tanks

o joyous grainy boulevards
black-&-white newsreels
o August of '44...

crowing this morning
commander-in-chief
touches down
mission accomplished

o history
o endless loop

o flight suit astride the deck,
o digital perfect photo op
off sunny San Diego

o words
brazing hope,
calling victory victory

the liberation of Baghdad

o cock a doodle do
cock a doodle do

o blood in the eye
blood on the bloody beak

come home to roost

Untitled

If we let our vision of the world
go forth

if we embrace our vision
entirely
our vision of the world

if we don't try to piece
together clever

no clever diplomacy
just war

if we just wage
total war

our children will sing
great songs of us

as of a radiance
resurrected
in the firmament

over a dead planet

DU Blues

DU
death row

wind blow

continents countries cities
flags
wind don't know
which way wind blow

whip up sandstorm
go wherever,
4 plus billion years
it got
to go forever

number the years
of forever

eat sleep fuck
uranium forever

X ray ever hour
the hours of a life
gone catch up forever

o swindled innocence of breath

o life condemned to kill
the life it come to save
save to rob it blind
gone wait alone together

DU DU DU
death row

wind blow

Arc

'The arc of the universe is long, but it bends toward justice.'
(Martin Luther King)

Like a dowsing rod reaching for water
the arc of the universe
bends toward justice –

but what if there is none?

nothing in the scheme of things
as far as we
in our lifetime see
bends, surely, toward justice

what may we do then
to bend
the arc of justice
back down to earth?

it won't be with speeches,
no one needs to strain, daydreaming
after words the wind blows through

attend instead
to the coming and going
of those who are better off
with justice, than without –

all the colours, shapes, customs
being done-to unto death

but don't lose yourself
in swirls of wreckage,
don't cling to debris

let the slop and flow
of white-capped dreamways
heaving onward through you

carry you along
as on a great wave cresting
an unfathomed sea of nameless peoples

who are bound to arrive somewhere

when you yourself arrive
cast up on the shore
imagine you've happened on
a folk tale. Imagine
you're in it: a noble
foundling from the sea,
the sea of peasants
storming the wicked lord's castle
saving everyone saving
the beauty of the bending universe
from the wrack and ruin
of the lord's stupidity,
his arrogance, his greed,
the dazzling panoply of his dementia
cutting words off
from the truth of the matter

imagine for that matter
Washington DC now
right now
is such a regime, its
lords ravage the countryside

imagine living this
imagine

seeing what we all see
feeling as we feel
having nothing left to prove
nothing more to discover
nowhere else to go

when you torch the manor house
ransack the cold cellar
tear down the whole rotten structure
imagine that

Donatello's Version

1

is unexpected:

the boy David
shamelessly naked,
one adorable leg
cocked at the knee

nonchalant
vulnerable
soft-bodied
a true killer

he wears his helmet
like a bonnet,
its pointy peak
garlanded with laurel leaves

2

the kid's a winner

little penis
big sword

standing astride
the craggy winged
head of the giant, Goliath

3

Goliath's head is peaceful,
his death like any death
is restful, untroubled
by desire or regret

4

David's skin glistens, obscurely
under a patina of melancholy

what's wrong with him

he should be dancing up and down
with joy

5

poor David
the good guy

victory is the worst thing
that could befall him

6

in the glass of his great victory,
through the loathsome mist
of world weariness

he sees himself
becoming *King* David

7

sees strings of victory
twining into distance
with strings of defeat

how he will conquer
and flee
how puff himself up
to hide

how he will dance around the sociopathic Saul

how marry, sire, beget
betrayals, adulteries,
murders, torture
prisoners raked
through the brick kiln

a weakness for poetry
will have him writing psalms
again and again –

for all he has won
by this great victory
is his own disaster:

his family, his kingdom, his people
tearing apart and apart

8

he will go through life
eating flesh by the fistful

choking on shadows

9

in the improbable blood
of his great victory

he sees all this
and is famished

The Donkeys

for Mondo

The donkeys scream but they don't run

to the war reporter on the scene
it makes no sense

foolish beasts, donkeys

beasts of burden
with no burden
but being here
aswarm
with war machines
in the waste of Iraq

soulless
beasts
lacking the faculty
of reason

too stupid to run,
too shaggy to think
there's somewhere to run to

I too must be stupid,
still here with no reason,
another dumb animal
stuck with the sense
that all is not lost
even as all is lost

the stubborn feeling
as all goes bad

the stubborn feeling

we're still here
on our tiny feet,
our droopy eyes
black crescents
veiling and unveiling
all the soul there is –
although, in fact, there is no soul

there *is* hope for us
although there's no hope

the situation is hopeless

as the reporter leaves that place
the donkeys are still screaming

Wild Trees

'The world was all before them, where to choose…'
(Milton, *Paradise Lost*, XII)

it was late in the day

we came upon
the obvious: crab apples,
blood clots of rusted fruit

these aroused in us
nostalgia
for what never existed
and never would

beyond, we noticed other trees
orchard apples abandoned
to the obsolescence
of prelapsarian desires –

hollow trunks
twisted, fruitless, leafless
sprouting twigs and twiglets
with slow, maniacal fury…

they explained nothing
illuminated nothing

    *

in this late light, explanation
insults intelligence

illumination blinds

    *

ahead: skeletal elms

scabrous trunks
lining a dirt road long after
the paved avenues of their heyday
have gone to rubble,
the trolley rails of our childhood
torn up

*

one after another
a line of crows by the water
flap flaps off –

the eschatological sheen
we can't see through
or into – because
it shines black,
blinding back at us
the death of everything –

is torn away
by flying black rags

not hurrying, exactly, but hustling
to get something done somewhere
who knows where or what

raucous, haranguing
the rawness of life

barking at one another

*

how unlike now the placid
strangeness of cows congregated
at the farthest, lowest corner of a pasture
not sitting or browsing, but
pressing some urgent concern
at an emergency meeting . . .

I'd no sooner inquire of that crowd
than of a skirmish line of crows
combing a meadow, tossing straws in the air

that way lies madness

    *

let the trees tree
madness

let the world world
I love it that the crabs
are inedible

the slender elms on either side,
fountains of stillness,
reach out to announce an arch over the mind

through which let the crows crow

    *

the bearing of those cows suggests
plain as day, showing their age
a Giotto fresco of Dominican friars,
massive brown robes and wide-brimmed hats
sheer bulk and colour
speaking nothing but big body language

    *

I myself came late to explanation

four years in a Dominican high school
I never thought to wonder
who was Saint Dominic?
the nuns never thought to tell us

not about Dominic
nor, later, Savonarola
stirring up the bonfire of the vanities –
not to be bought off
by the pope's offer of a cardinal's hat

'A red hat? I want a hat of blood.'

> *so hanged*
> *& burned*

*

the nuns had no more to do with that
than Mary did with Joseph –

or did they know better
than try to explain it

*

because wherever they turned, they saw
we all did, under the same dispensation
the Virgin Mary on a pedestal
arms spread wide, and low,
palms up in perpetuity,
robes blue and white
above the bank of vigil candles,
flames drafting over the glass rims
licking the gloom above
the glowing red cups they were set in

her bare foot still
crushes the serpent's head,
her expressionless complexion
still looks
time into cold, unwrinkled space
gone straight to heaven
without passing through death
as even Jesu did, I mean
that Mary, she was one *wild* tree

who in her muteness
as darkness flies up
gives away nothing, except
the endlessness of nothing,
hence the futility of longing

Mary, in whom
all questions died before they could come to mind

Babble

it starts with Hazel, my mother

a factory worker
looking to dress up
go out, have fun

hollering screaming

threw things
cleaned house like a demon
threw everyone out

you'll be sorry when I'm gone
you'll see!

nothing explained
nothing to ponder
no moral

*

nothing, ever,
approaching a conversation

*

it starts with Hazel then
who could be anyone
crouched at the edge of the bed
like a feral animal

3 pocketbooks on one arm,
crumbs scattered

hair crimped in a tight perm
dyed *Frivolous Fawn*
by Revlon
or Clairol

who is this person?

if looks could kill
I'd be wounded

*

the place reeks of bodily fluids
at war
with antiseptic solutions

*

I don't know how I got to this party
I'm not working overtime

factory or party, whatever
she wants out
a ride home
shoving the walker
like a balky child

no one want money?
what's the matter with them?

waving a $5 bill,
the tiny flag she counts on
to get her out of here

if she makes it to the far door
an alarm goes off

*

baa baa baa baa baa
behind the screen –

Irene, a fetal curl
dying of nothing but *old*,
babbling gargling *old old argh*
like a rockslide

old means
something falls away from you
and keeps falling

history is shit

＊

how did we ever
leap into speech?

or did it break out like a ruckus
spilling into the street

regardless it goes on saying
old exhausted beating at air
still creeping up on us

Socrates having drunk hemlock
given unto death
beyond death
questions still –
his voice *tweaks*
bat-like, sounding us out

Pan, another troublemaker
totally out of control
without a word still wreaks
waves of havoc

cosmic inertia
drags birth screams
through dying gasps

hauls death rattles
through agonies of rumour
where nothing is forgotten
because nothing can be forgotten

the logorrhea of eternal life
goes on and on at a party
that is no longer a party

*

Irene
slips into the unquiet stupor
we call sleep

Socrates doesn't concern her,
nor Greek

it's anyone's guess
what she has to do with Pan,
she could be his ancestor

*

for Hazel, English itself
is Greek

in the language she speaks
nothing has its own name, just
that thing! that thing there!
arthritic jabber, jabbing
a crooked finger

still she knows a thing or two
Socrates doesn't

*she knows she doesn't know
how she got to this party,
she knows no one in this place
will give her a ride home*

hence the family photos
banished from the windowsill
the paper bag mashed to the floor
the half box of crackers
the spectacles cast down

damned
for abandoning her

*

Hazel you can't go home

the house has been sold

*

and so, and so, what is life
is also
the abandonment of life

what's left of Hazel's
heart muscle
flutters to relax
in the slipstream of morphine

they call this 'comfort care'
this quiet dying

on this barely 4' 10" female
the factory crumpled hands
are monumental

her thick gray hair
undyed, unmangled
flows away from her face
radiating out over the pillow

her ashes falling away
from their fury

*

Irene snores, still,
through death, life, the hereafter

wadded up in the darkness of life

*

what are words for

can anyone really tell
one thing from the other
without pointing?

or is it *blah blah blah*
all Pan all the time
a 24 hour talk show
saying nothing real loud
and mean

*

you just know Socrates

the first and maybe last
extractor of human truths
from truisms
more septic than lies

is throwing up his hands

*

still if we could get past
English, past Greek

if we could crash
eternally collapsed time,
the one party we weren't invited to,
the party of matted loins
shrieking feeling
for god knows what lips
blind smashing all to bits
dizzied, with no regard
for anything or anyone

we too might find ourselves
losing ourselves

with Socrates
his moral logic
the deft limbs of it
lost, and yet
found, in the entourage
of the bestial god Pan crushing
sentiment, scattering
qualms, family, civilizations
crackers, money, photographs
in one ecstatic panicked millisecond of babble –

there, in the babble of awful truth

we might leave be
the Irene thing
the toothless mouth hole
dying endlessly of *old*
gargling ancient gravel beds

might leave the Hazel thing
that was somebody's mother
with 3 pocketbooks on one arm
and no ride home from the party
the factory, the final hospital
she never did know how she got to

...leave ourselves, too,
strangers and alone together
who in the end could not tell
one from the other

the voices were so mixed up

          *

having shrugged off, then
language that pushes us along
like naughty children

we might meet ourselves
beyond the babble
of what was called humanity

engaging, for sake of argument,
in Pan Socratic dialogue
making no sense at all,
making all the sense in the world,

bright children growing
old with Pan

feeling in our own bones
the aching bones
of this very minor god

wrapped in his rank skin
suffused with the smell of it,
wandering corridors
leaning on our walker
agitated, asking questions
too simple for answers
too hard

how did we come to this

waving the worthless flag
the worthless money
of words that lost their meaning,
looking for a ride home

Woman in Black Chador, Running

the head held so high
it tilts back
a balancing act, running

eyes watery watering

like the girl in Vietnam
last century, only yesterday
still with us in a famous photo
out of her element still
throwing her head back
the same way
running naked, trailing napalm vapours
too wispy to be visible

this one is not naked though,
this is no girl
the other was slender
this is round, soft, fifty-ish
this has a homely oval face
wrapped head to toe
in black fabric

this is 2003
this is *this* century

running from nothing anyone can see
from no napalm
by Macy's on O'Farrell Street

with no neck running,
no shoulders,
fists tucked up
under the chin

head into body streaming
its unbroken shroud

like a fish out of water
limbs fanning, gasping

the eyes of the fish
wide with feeling,
preposterous feeling

as though a bomb has dropped
on O'Farrell Street

Scleroderma

Water you crave water
membranes thicken
the ravening mouth

you're coming down
with something
can a face hurt?
your face hurts
and teeth,
teeth hurt
but never like this

tongue's bunched,
shoulders ratchet
pain
there's no turning back

the more stone-like
this body that is not you
the greater the agony

you would resolve this
paradox but not now

now is no time for musing

the joints
with instinctive wisdom
contract,
set for impact

skin thickens, has to,
itself is all the armour it has

liver hardens, lungs
crumple, papery

who puts a hand
on your bared chest
feels the death
crinkling under it

what's left of heart
arcane machinery, pumps
incomprehensible fluid
to no end

primeval organs
are last to go,
the digestive tract
intestines
genitalia

the moistness of future
turned off
like a faucet

now you are petrified,
you have survived

it is your destiny
to be shut up alive

you are your own
headstone: struck dumb
in this headstone dump
of leanings and crumblings
coming to nothing

you can still hear them, the silences
stone histories
stone schools
stone freedoms
stone laws
stone soldiers
stone news
stone this
stone that

everywhere

the silences
of stones that die
hurtling through space

Resurrection

for Arlene

It's like the Resurrection, you say
waking feeling skin

you mean
Signorelli's *Resurrection*:
bodies flexing, stretching belief
against one gorgeous, overarching
metaphysical manifestation
of human anatomy

you who know
we won't really be resurrected

when we die we die

yet now when we awaken
after all these years
in our own flesh, which
no matter how old
feels so good

the way, in the fresco,
the translucent-skinned
muscular dead feel

for resurrection
we imagine only
caressing one another

here   now

where art is no more
than life, realizing itself

Except for Lazarus

it is a fact, we die

it is also a fact
however old we die
the correct age for resurrection
theologically, but humanly too
is 33

the prime of life

the age Jesus
died and lived again
like a corn god
historically documented,
a god in a time
like this time –

except for Lazarus
wretched in rags
no one is resurrected
into decrepitude

no one, except

in a time like this
whose gods resurrect
only Lazarus
the walking grave

Lazarus on Lazarus
faceless heaps
of urine and blanket grease
bundled in doorways

human beings
burrowing for warmth
like so many despoiled
holes in time

by such signs we see
the gods of our time
bring death to life

that is the miracle

The Hamlet Mess

Everyone rewrites Hamlet,
even the chimpanzees.
Well not the whole Hamlet, not chimps,
but at least the beginning.
For them, that itself is an achievement.
Hunting and pecking on an old typewriter
one day they find
they have a hairy finger in the Hamlet pie.
There's a play about this,
a thinking person's *Planet of the Chimps*.

Nearly everyone takes a stab at it.
Not to get it right
– after all, Hamlet himself didn't –
but to get it wrong in the right way,
the way that suits them.

Take the Arab Hamlet, Hamlet
without make-up, dying.
Of course his whole life is dying.
He finds out secrets that are killing him
and blows them up. Like Ur-Hamlet does.
And lives in a rotting state, or none at all,
where the physical world is so metaphysical
living is a contradiction in terms.
'Don't bring the curtain down,' he pleads,
as though he had curtains, as though
he could die before he's blasted away
by the lies that make up the Hamlet play –
as though he weren't caged up
in reality, the last sky, beyond
the playhouse of the fictional Hamlet's
dinky stage with its dark, crampt wings.

Naturally the Israeli Hamlet is proscribed
by the Israelis. He exists, yes
but only on a list, a sacred scroll

which may not be revealed –
an exceedingly Hamlet-like predicament.

The Israeli Hamlet may be the purest
Hamlet on God's troubled earth.

The Polish Hamlet is another kettle of
stewing. He tells ghost stories to children
(he's the only Hamlet who has them)
stories about a rat behind the arras
while the kids wonder, what's an arras?
Him talking talking, yet
thinking thinking, not telling them
he's the Polish Hamlet, it's *he* who dwells on
the milk-smooth thighs of the queen mother–
keeping mum, too, about the poor mad girl
the English Hamlet looked to death.

As for that question about hatpins
and choosing to be or not to be
it is, he says, a crude stupid joke
'to the man of today.' To get the joke
though, we'd have to be Polish
coming back again & again
plodding, utterly hopeless,
into what passes for the world.

The German Hamlet on the other hand . . .
but which German Hamlet?
There are so many.
Often the German Hamlet isn't Hamlet
but Ophelia whose scream tunnels the water,
her spell compels a bullet
to shatter against a willow leaf.

But typically, stereotypically,
the German Hamlet is a machine
smashing its well-oiled image to bits.
Now that's a Hamlet. It rips
idiotic Elizabethan questions

into fustian scrap.
And drinks on it.

Which leads straight to the Russian Hamlet!
There's a vast, deep hinterland.
We will never run out of Russian Hamlets.
Like the original, they fidget. Carp.
Here's one loves the role, but not the play.
He wants the script changed!

But by far, hands down,
the most fascinating, pathetic,
feelingly ridiculous Russian Hamlet
sleeps in the same room as you
but in another bed. He doesn't sleep
of course, nor do you, but goes over
his shallow, insignificant, worthless
unoriginal life with such great energy
and passion, it startles the provincial
pomposity stranded in the next room.
Strangely, you wish he wouldn't shut up,
this bundle of nerve-ends, but he does.
In the morning, he's gone.

Doubtless there are other Hamlets.
Argentinean, Nigerian, Indonesian,
a Japanese in a video arcade playing
killer games with the state of his dreams
and, possibly, the state of the princess.
But if so, I don't know them.
Or did, and forgot.

One thing is certain: only the Americans
do not write, or rewrite, Hamlet.
If they do it's a family film
with murder and incest, nothing huge.
Yet how imagine a Hamlet who does not
agonize over picky little things all balled up
in the state of the world? What world
might an American Hamlet agonize over?

And what's to ponder, or notice, about
a billow of clothing, some weeds,
a glimpse of flesh and hair
drifting down a river?

Nor do they agonize
over the ghosts of their fathers
or worry what's rotten, or what to kill, even though
like the young Prince Hamlet, wherever they pass
something bad happens, and after that
something worse.

Hamlet himself, only just realizing as much,
is puzzled to discover his own hand
in his own blood.

In Wildered Dust

squatters in the wildered dust
where people once lived...

they've crashed
their own death camp

mistaking it
for a victory party

Star Chamber

by tradition
justice wears a blindfold,
sword in one hand
scales in the other

sometimes, a book
in the crook of her arm
or under the armpit

but print blurs
words
swamp with ink

ink
darkens the blood
words drown in

      *

sky is a dome of stars
with no constellation
for justice

when we look up
into the darkness
that's best to see in
justice is what we feel
the absence of –

only Libra, whose
superbly balanced scales
may not be disturbed
by justice or injustice,
      remains –
to take our eyes off
the grounds we're standing on

      *

to constellate justice
we'd have to wield the sword
write off the law books
unhook the fulcrum
from the scales

we have no scales to weigh
the metaphysical difference
the palpable indifference
between innocence and guilt

    *

justice being blind
needs no blindfold

still we bind it tight
on principle, or for
poetic truth pull
a sack over its head

    *

as if justice were a person
and not
the personification of a system

tearing off archaic robes

dropping the blindfold
throwing caution to the gods
slipping out of fiction
into fatigues

tugging on the rubber gloves
which fit
like unfeeling skin

to strip prisoners
down to the cocks
she will be pointing at
for ever now

her wretched pathos
wanting only to please
her, & our, masters –

because we *are* her,
she knows us,
the whole gang of us
staring back through the camera
into posterity

in our dream
of unimaginable innocence
siccing the dogs on

＊

we will think about this
a long while, and then

we will stop thinking

They

Sadr City, 28 August 2004

took him inside the house
detained
his family on the patio

cut off the plastic cuffs
shot him in the head, twice,
dragged him out

his wife
hysterical, wailing
throwing dirt in the air
beat on herself with both hands

they watched, shocked
she placed her baby
on the bleeding body

this had not occurred
to the video wars
racketing the screens
of their video games

the yellow ribbons
neatly looped and swallow-tailed
on trees and cars, boding
their soldiers coming home
had envisioned nothing
as mad

as a baby's blind warmth
on a man's corpse

Codex Gitmo

*'I believe there are police; but the law here must be so different
I can't imagine what the criminals must be like.'*
(Rimbaud, 'Cities II')

1

justice hoods justice,
cages it

2

under armed escort
a blindfolded animal

no charges no
evidence
to fabricate this
new world wilderness

3

an entire nation
throwing up its constitution
had to be numbed, gutted,
the machinations of its heart
pulled out, reconstructed
still pumping blood
to police this zoo

4

as usual
among animals
it's impossible to tell
what is criminal

we know only innocence
is out of the question

Dies Ire

My era tells me bluntly:
you do not belong.
I answer bluntly:
I do not belong.
(Adonis)

on the day of wrath
in orange jumpsuits
we keep the faith

heads bowed,
eyes blacked out,
made to kneel
broken-minded
in the gravel of eternal night

eternal night the god
we are given to pray to
on burning knees

Strange Words

'Whoever was tortured, stays tortured.'
(Jean Améry)

blindfolded
bent over a table
pants pulled down
stick shoved up
the rectum

strange word, rectum
stranger by the day

unreasonable residue
of rectify and rectitude
not right, but narrow

I couldn't scream
but when I did
I couldn't stop

how will the poem
approach this

strange word, poem
stranger than rectum

a panhandler
suspiciously well-dressed:
spare a word?
a syllable or two?
speaking what
might be Greek

looking for something
real, but not too, a little
something the poem can use

yet passing through
this netherworld
of beastly silence
the scream goes on,
spares nothing

There is No Truth to the Rumour

there is no truth to the rumour
the Constitution's
a goddamned piece of paper

it's not vegetable, but animal
dressed as parchment –

invented in Pergamon
in not yet Turkey
3rd century BCE
when the papyrus ran out

Ionian Greeks called sheets of it
diphtherai, or 'skins'

by the time of Herodotus
writing on skins was common

Assyrians and Babylonians
in what for now is called Iraq
were already writing on skins

writing and rewriting
past traces of earlier writing
on recycled skins
they'd scrubbed and scoured

they wrote what they believed
mattered
on something meant to last

rabbinic books weren't books
but scrolls of parchment, as
were, later, early Islamic texts

great civilizations as living cultures
writing themselves on skin

writing rewriting
laws, histories, religions, all
on cured skin: split
sheepskin, goatskin, cowhide,
horsehide, squirrel and rabbit

aborted calf foetuses
hairless through and through
as is the skin of angels
would be reserved
for especially precious stuff

yet regardless of grade, without exception,
skin being mostly collagen,
the water in ink or paint
would melt it slightly
creating a raised bed for the writing

like welts on a body
showing what's been done to it

even today, to write on parchment
or colour it
the tiniest bit watery
is to bring all this doing up

each writing a rewriting
overwriting the life of skin

so if its breath is gone, its muscles
having lost all sense of purpose
bereft of heart and liver, still
in the heat and humidity
of human and meteorological exertion
it buckles, shifts, sweats and squirms

uplifting a little,
like from a death bed,
giving lie to the rumour
the Constitution is a piece of paper
damned or not

because, even dead, it will let us know
this was a living matter
that was being painted up, written off on
chewed by dogs, and lied over

Boxcars

'a light unto the nations'

1

Christmas '43
I'm six everything exists

     in pristine space

    the brand new
Lionel electric train on its oval track
speeds through the straightaway
  slows
at the curve
    snakes away
in a jumble of colourful boxes

...reappears
as a steam engine,
a ponderous black beast
    yoked
to rough wooden boxcars
bucolic as oxcarts

the older I will get
the earlier the times I will live in

2

the duration of the war
creaking the spur line behind our house
    real trains crawl by nightly
      whooing
        through my bedroom
boxcars of munitions, rifles, side arms
Colt, High Standard, Winchester's, Marlin Firearms . . .

V-J Day
    with a clothesline rope
we hanged Tojo from a cherry tree
and burned the carcass

the trains went away . . .

    I slept
        to the gurgled *cooing*
of pigeons under the eaves, clearing their throats

days on end we scavenged the barely used tracks
    like scrap yard dogs
in a heaven on earth of coal-blue cinders
cratered, razory–
    we kept
getting skins nicked, sneakers
torn, not noticing
    we were so excited!
on the iron path to the ends of the known world

    all wonder ran
between the backyards and the slow curve of the tracks

    3

when was it boxcars began to fill
with rumours of Jews?

quietly, nondescript, they were gone
    like sunflower seeds
shoveled into a mouth of blackened teeth
swallowed up in concentration camps

not consecrated, yet, as death camps

decades later, no one could think boxcars
without thinking Jews

4

Saturday matinée us kids
        licorice sticky
watch the Pathé news

The Eyes Of The World
one monster lens
        reaches into the darkness
we nestle in–the Voice of the World
bigger and heavier than life itself
is rolling over us

GIs LIBERATE THE CAMPS!

we daren't breathe
as soldiers unravel limbs skin bones hair,
lift the striped pyjamas, stack
carefully, awkward, not wanting to touch
        or break
the fragile staring things inside them
onto truck beds

bewildered are the soldiers
        in helmets,
eyes fixed, trying not to stare
at the bewilderment of the pyjamas

the little round caps set squarely
on the tops of shaved heads

5

under the heaps of cheap baggy cottons
the broad-striped bags of bones
there is a prior life,
the life before this

hiding, holding its breath
in old photographs: stiff poses
        estranged
under the merciful haze of sepia . . .

no grace descends
         on the grainy photo faces
weighed down, now, in hopelessly old-fashioned clothing,
the layers, they wear, of all they can carry,
the murmurous shuffle of a stadium crowd
that could in a panic crush itself

but doesn't–
         living still, still willing
ordinary everyday reality, they are still
in their hearts
people people under a pall of silence:
         these faces
         like tremulous leaves
curled whitely, sensing change in the weather
of a place with no trees

                6

I'm 16 watching an SS officer's
         home movie–
a 'short' thrown in unannounced
at the art house a block from the school
I'm playing hooky from–
         caught now
                  off guard
by the nakedness, the sizes and ages
    the so many shades of white
of normal healthy women lined up for the showers

what's shocking is
         what's shocking:
they're supposed to be starving
but aren't

they're healthy! why kill them?

the kid watching this
         is struck
half a century older thinking

what if they'd been sick
all skin, bones & eyes?

because it wasn't the murder
        got to him, but
the meaninglessness of it

how he imagines
        ghastly death
cannot comprehend bodies
so banal, so lined up and *out there*
like it's nothing nothing's happening

the naked women
the soldiers in their uniforms
        guarding them
in the skincrawling abyss of their decorum
are still as period pieces
at the end of the known world

the soldiers not staring but looking
off, distracted
as though daydreaming

7

how is it
the undressed bodies of long dead human beings
turn spectral, like dirty air
        catching the light

half-buried
awful treasure

8

mornings in the mirror
        I see
a daguerreotype
staring back at me

not really my face
but an unreconstructed
          history–
the obsolescent technology
of eyes, nose, lips
light and shadow

breathing in, out, in, out,
the unsorted humanity

of dirty air

                    9

what is it, '67? 1967?
I'm thirty, nothing is pristine

when I look for them again
              they've fled!
taking their nakedness with them

the train so long now
no one can see the end of it

boxcars loom, battered walls on wheels
the great clanking segments
passing passing
pushing pulling jerking rattling
brushing rusting weeds, leaving
the pennies we had laid atop the rails
flattened, shiny & faceless . . .

child's play gives way
to a chain gang of Memorial Horrors
          hitched together
on a round-the-world rail tour

like a milk train
          it stops
at every town it rumbles through,
a bloody road show,

chronic reproach
like original sin, determined never again
to be born in innocence
            coming and going
as a haunting refrain
never again never again never again
                the burden
whose final destination is a mystery . . .

on the scarred, implacable sides of the boxcars
    HOLOCAUST
in thick black Gothic script
stares out, near yet distant

                        within
human remains lie scattered, withered,
boneyards dug up to people
            re-people
museums of death with the uncomprehending dead
finding themselves yet again
            dragged from sleep
to be taken where now? to what end?

they had not dreamed of this life
after life

                    10

more night, more fog, rolls in

the natural light of the world
obsessed
            with an agenda
turns, merely, to lighting . . .

the world was coming down with something
feverish
            film noir-ish
always on the run from something
            obliterating

all, falling into
a bottomless pit of feeling without feeling

my heart was pounding
       caught
red-handed in the immolation
of human history

HOLOCAUST
    descending
dead ending everything and everyone into something
        shameful and shameless
came howling like a soul afire
burning the worlds away

11

I came to in a boxcar,
there was nowhere else to be

others there were, also transported
amid muffled
        coughing, breathing
trying not to make a scene

...winding through the '50s, '60s, '80s
        Y2K fantasm
switch-backed into the '70s, tunnelled from light
       to dark & then
the '40s '30s vortex
shabby, breaking broken glass–

HOLOCAUST fires gasped sucking
air out of the air, the engine seemed
      to stoke itself
with the remains of ordinary people,
the long dead, first, in shrouds of clothing,
then the sad-eyed, the darkly artful, the sullen
       leaving behind
the striped stick figures in terrible baker's caps
serving now no further purpose

the rest of us
speechless, rattled,
      jerked
every which way,
we too were being consumed
      broken down
in the belly of a great ancient conquering army,
      an armoured column
of boxcars, logistical genius, caught up
in the triumphal march of misery
     over future,
over the simple recognition
of human

     surpassing all

the peasant holocausts along the way,
the unprepossessing ethnic cleansings
of centuries left speechless,
nameless

eyes, noses, lips
never again
to relate a human face

rolling past all that now
       swaying toward sleep
     past insignificant bloodlettings,
        the merest whispers of them
sinking into marshes deserts jungles steppes
walled-off parts of cities
where they are heard from hardly ever

and then, never

clickety-clacking
clickety-clacking

clickety-clacking

I must have dozed off, everyone must have,
     next we know
our sleep is a nightmare, it wants
desperately to end, but can't–
     every bend
          rocking side to side
is a turn for the worse, the dead
are condemned to deliver themselves
over and over
as scripted or on demand

the Holocaust local looms
    like fate
a global munitions train

train we'd thought stopped running
    that eve
we hanged Tojo from the cherry tree
soaked in kerosene

running now over everything

over Guatemalan
     or were those Mayan
anyway kids, mothers, Nicaraguans, Salvadorans, Chileans

black South Africans unloading the arms
that will kill themselves

and then, I swear,
     the boxcar walls were plastered with American flags,
we'd hitched a ride home in a cargo plane,
     the GIs in cardboard boxes like freight draped in Old Glory
          to be offloaded, fork-lifted onto a loading dock –
American Holocaust flags streaming someplace still
          where all the blacks were gone
converted enlisted drowned or locked up somewhere
with the scraps of Indians flushed through everyone's blood

finished off in film
                    swept away
into a dreamland without clocks or windows,
                            paroled to casinos
            as in a time travel machine
creating its own warp
on its own track

coursing now
over Cambodian skulls with ID photos, through Rwandans
o god Rwandans in '59, '63, '93, '94, '95
                    huddled inside a church
while out in the great beyond of all that is precious
            begging to be extracted from this earth
machetes take their sweet time awaiting
            the decency of dark
to come in

                    13

cries & cryings brushed aside
by boxcars

                    boxcars

                            boxcars

                    14

even to speak this
is unspeakable

to speak
of Sudanese women and children in the gorgeous wraps
of National Geographic –
                            skeletal young girl, lustrous skin
stretched tight on bone frame like a black paper kite
            grounded, staring
through airless umber haze of dust and flies
                    tells as nothing else
            how fantastic how beautiful creation is

to speak of the atrocity
of the aesthetic

because beauty shows through
even this
the way a column of smoke
            gushes up
on its own exhaustion
wreathing an agony of shadows
            Hiroshima
                      human
fingers ignite like flares
dead black pieces flaking onto the road
leading to the river

because this too is unspeakably human

the women are war-raped
as other women
         of other colours
the same colour
sing the rapists on

because how heady are
the rails singing and clicking beneath our feet

clickety-clacking

Congo Congo Congo
the eternity of Congo
bloodied running on

Nigeria
Chechnya
clickety clickety
Sudan
boiling flesh Uzbekistan

speechless bodies
flashing by on either side

metal skinning metal
rocking
into the 21st century

its children
the moving target
its children
its children
its children

locked into
the racketing
boxcars of Holocaust

15

look! what should have been
light is darkness

longthening
        Cossack haunted
shadows of the Holocaust
rampage across and across
the Holyland they dreamed
in darkness
        dreamed
driving two-leggèd beasts
to extinction . . .

16

in this dream, your dream,
we exist as *present absentees*
        insects
            in perennial rubble
under a heaven of unforgiving genesis

whatever tells of us
who used to be human
        is walled-up

with all of future inside it
& crushed
      like an eggshell
by bulldozers bigger than a house

17

your dream is a nightmare
because we are in it

we crowd the streets between curfews
your tank clanks through
    slowly
sprays us with DDT
as though we're another species

we could be another species

we were born in boxcars
the bad faith of boxcars,
the *carte blanche* of boxcars,
bundled under munitions
side by side
with dug up naked bones

our fathers mothers grandparents
uncles aunts, kids old as
stones, as dirt, as names, oranges, hearts
older than histories
are heaved up into them
      as wanderers
in battered trunks called *the demographic problem*

as who on earth isn't
a demographic problem

look at us,
we carry no weight
    we miscarry
your missiles in the marketplace
we, who are the perishables

with us, now, the ghosted boxcars of the Holocaust careen
                 so screamingly light
the bad dream gone really bad
they threaten to fly, fly, dragged
                             off the rails, to crash
this only life on earth we are passing through

because when our species ends
yours does too

The Angel of History

'His eyes are staring, his mouth is open, his wings are spread.'
(Walter Benjamin)

blown backwards
into the future

he beholds only
the past
dragging after him

what a catastrophe
the furious wind
hurls at his feet

helpless before it

his wings are spread–
fanned flat
with the sharp snap
of terrified sails

how will he fold them
feather on feather
before the torrent
of shock waves from paradise?

him
on his wretched wings
helpless to help
anyone
or anything

what he shouts
is spittle
torn from his mouth

himself, ever only
a single breath ahead
of where he has been

where even now

the surge of broken bodies
is breaking over him

filling his eyes, his mouth, his ears
with creaturely whispers

crushing with love the wings
that have caught him up
in so much misery

Dadalab

1

the beginnings of dada
were not the beginnings
of an art
but of a disgust

so Tristan Tzara in 1922

dada came to be
the shrine of a urinal
–fountain of poverty–
signed into an art museum

a pig in an army uniform
floating overhead,
the Prussian archangel
swimming through air
kicking its little boots, grunting
'High from the Heavens I Come'

Hugo Ball nonsense syllables
dada babble
blowing up like body parts
shoulders of words hands arms legs
of words
fleeing the Great War

weird humor

scatting lines
in the sand
between art and pissy death

2

dada judo turns
newspapers, cripples, ticket stubs
into dada ads

not to disavow art, but
to shred its
illusory transcendence

to make visible the violence
of business as usual,
its chaos and hypocrisy

laughing like mad

dada was all for
vomiting itself
out of the Great War

3

Janco Dada Museum
the heart of Ein Hod
is also built upon
art thrown up by war

a not so great war

Ein Hod = Ayn Hawd
a village in 1949
the Jews drove the Arabs
out of

its haunting emptiness
evoked, then, biblical ruins–
here was a heaven-sent
construction site
to mystify the bounds
of art and life

to metamorphose
dada, the art of war,
into a bubbly art movement
where, in the Dadalab,
art concocts reality–

everything is possible,
objects like a refrigerator
or a table or picture
can go through walls,
a pot becomes an animation apparatus,
the imagination spreads its wings
and soars ...

says the museum brochure

and in truth, in this
art that's a kind of anti-art
everything *is* possible

the Arabs who squat on a hill
a mile or so from home
live without electricity
without water, without a road,
without wings

imagine living without wings,
and yet they do

as animation apparatuses,

present absentees
like tables or pictures
that can go through walls

because the ends of dada
like its beginnings
are not the ends of an art
but of a disgust

troubling the ghosts of Ayn Hawd
whom museum walls go through

Qana

where the wedding was
where water turned to wine
where the best was saved
for last

shsh   they're trying to sleep
in the dark wood
of dreamless dreaming–
coughing farting snoring sighing
turning over

where the wedding was
the rolling storm
that is not a storm
flies over

it doesn't feel much
to drop a bomb–
a slight bump
under the wing

the thing is done–

their deaths
like little yapping dogs
rush out
into the nerve-endings of the universe

the bodies stay put,
impossibly still

so it was said in school
Macbeth doth murder sleep–
with so much life to kill
there's no room for sleep

in Qana
where the wedding was
those who sleep, die

the future of sleep
is buried alive

in Qana where the wedding was
the murdered in their sleep
wake, just long enough to die
to become the woods
where the wedding was . . .

they are on the move now,
which is impossible

these impossible dead
growing out of their deaths
into an army of trees

Oceania

how huge how powerful
the masks the shields
the painted wood
war club

ornamented skulls
cassowary feathers
eye sockets
pooling
a mosaic of shells
how small how shiny
the forehead
polished as ivory

ancestral
spirit carved paddles

a bone dagger
the handle top-knot
cascading hair
to hide the hand
that held it

I say that hand
is here
lit by late afternoon
light and shadow
swimming through dust

my own hand
with its veins
its speckled reddishness
labeled *human*

what is human–
a species of matter
cutting the water in long canoes
stroking the spume of passion, beauty, blood

terrified, terrifying

Atahualpa Death Prayer

'Apu Inka Atawallpaman'
(Quechua, Anon. date uncertain)

1

What sick rainbow is this
stealing in, so black?
For Cuzco's enemies
a false dawn dances,
a hailstorm of disease
beating on everyone

2

Time and again
my heart
sensed it coming –
and I, sunk in dreams
fitful, half felt
the nasty blue fly of death

3

In one omen the sun
went out, paling
shrouding the corpse of Atahualpa.
And with his death his lineage
diminished
in the blink of an eye.

4

Grim enemies
cut off his head,
already the river of blood
breaks up branching out

5

Already his strong teeth gnaw
anguish they can't stop,
the brilliant eyes of the great Inca
cloud over

6

Now the great heart of Atahualpa
turns bitter cold, now
throughout his four dominions
they're shouting their lungs out

7

Thick mist misting down
amasses darkness.
Mother moon withdraws into herself
as if wishing to be reborn,
everyone's busy hiding themselves,
remorseful

8

Earth refuses to take in
its master–as if
mortified by the corpse
of one who loved it,
loathe to devour
its lord

9

Now the hardness of rock
gives way, hollowing,
the river roaring sorrow
swells to overflowing

10

Tears held back rush forth,
river carries them off.
Who human has not wept
for a loved one?
What child would not be
by its father's side?
Moaning, heavy heart struck
joyless

11
What virgin dove would not
care for who loves her?
And what wild stag, dying, doesn't let
its heartbeats keep it going?

12
Tears of blood
torn from joy, reflect
in shining drops
the corpse,
heart softened,
blood bathed in his country's lap

13
Those touched in passing
by his masterful hands,
those enfolded in
the wings of his heart,
those protected
by the fine mesh of his chest,
wail with the unbridled cries
of inconsolable widows

14
Colorful women congregate
but dressed in black,
the sun priest has wrapped himself
in his most dark cloak,
common people line up
by the graves

15
Death spreads. Sorrow stuns.
Tears of the Queen Mother
burst like spring freshets
over the yellowing corpse.
Her face is cold, pallid.
Her mouth speaks:

16

Where will you in exile
find rest, out of my sight,
leaving our land
abandoned to suffering,
you from my heart
cut out forever?

17

Regardless rooms of promised treasure,
the foreign enemy, your captors,
by nature
rapacious voracious carried on
like snarly beasts in a mad rush.
Those you gave
an easy life with gold and silver
gave you death.

18

Captured
you lavished on them all they desired,
but with your death in Cajamarca
everything stopped.
In your arteries
blood crusts.
Eyes blur. Your look
dissolves into the dark side
of the brightest star.

19

Who feels for you weeps, wanders, runs
after your well-loved soul–
your fevered troubled heart
howls
breaking off from the indignity
of your perishing

20

Your gold sedan chair dismantled,
your throne
its canopy woven of gold threads
shredded, is handed out as spoils

21
Ruled by heaped up punishments
cut to the quick
stupefied, estranged, without justice
isolated
weighing how our bodies have no shadows
we cry
to no one to appeal to
ourselves alone together, talking crazy

22
Will your heart allow us
great Inca
to be wandered every which way
scattered
at large, to be by others
ground underfoot?

23
Open your clear-seeing eyes,
open them!
reach out your hands
most giving,
and with this good sign
leave us strong

The Long Defeat

and when the gods are gone
into the long, drunken night–
gods of the globe
drunk with blood, drunk with money,
with hatred of life

we will go after them
into the same night

7 THEY ARE 7

the seven demons of Akkadia

swimming the shallows of the sea
exhausting the breath
of sky after sky

encrypted in wedge-shaped
writings on the walls
of a Mesopotamian temple

deciphered by Winckler
the German archeologist,
translated as poetry
by Konstantin Balmont
the Russian symbolist:

they are not of men, nor of women,
they have no wives, they sire no sons,
like the wind they wander, like nets
they cast themselves over everyone,
they are evil, they know no charity,
they know no shame,
they do not hear our prayers,
they do not hear our pleas

so moved Prokofiev,
already moved
by the October Revolution,
he composed 7 THEY ARE 7
with three lines of his own–

they wither heaven and earth,
they imprison countries like an iron gate,
they grind people as people grind grain

*

at the time it was said
how his music will sound 10 years from now
is an open question,
but on this evening his work
made a powerful impression:
it is huge and rather horrible and primitive–
the most effective composition by Prokofiev
we have heard

more astounding today
anyone anywhere in the world
cannot help
but hear these demon gods

as primitive and as horrible

locking up country after country,
withering its heavens
torturing its earth

Rings of Saturn

billions of stars

long time
    vastness
exploding over us,
eternity
scratching its ass

the gods
eat their children

we
their watchdogs bark
wordspeak
through watchdog teeth

bristling
slavering
at the end of this terrible chain

Isaac

It's not true
Isaac was an innocent

who could survive
such innocence?

he knew on the instant
he'd been set up
as a sacrificial lamb
or goat
or adolescent ram

the kindling he'd gathered
the stake
the ropes
the homely paraphernalia
all were ready, waiting

their silence calling to him
like old Kronos'
hairy mouth, tearing itself open
to devour his own sons

so Abraham himself
knife in hand, waiting
by the god's command
stood calling him to the pyre
hurry hurry
to run the knife across
the young animal
Isaac's throat

and yet . . .

what was Isaac saying?
what was he doing
dissolving the blade

honed to a whisper
in Abraham's own blood?
the blood of an old man!
his own father!

whatever passed then
through Abraham
rushed
blacker than his own blood
into bitter earth . . .

This is the true story
that may not be told
in anyone's lifetime,
surely not in the lifetime
of Abraham's god
the god, also, of Isaac

Anthology of Rapture

What are they looking for
running to the summit of lost time?

Hundreds of people vaporized
instantly
are walking in mid-air

We didn't die
we skipped over death in a flash we became spirits

Give us a real a human death
as if we'd existed

not this that is less than a field of paper cranes

the shadow of one man among hundreds
engraved on stone steps

Why am I printed on stone?
Where did my flesh go, without its shadow?

Where will shadow go
no way up
no way down
these steps, feet gone
shadowing shadow on stone

The 20th century is a myth
frozen in fire–
a woman's fingers
flare like candles,
who will blow them out?

Who will free this stone
from its shadow?

It isn't that the threat of the bomb is great
but that the earth is small

how is it the 20th century passed
        ...leaving behind
a rag of skin, on which
the victim's face appeared

I've shed the face of a human being
I'm stuck to a piece of gauze
but that don't stop me screaming

Between my teeth uranium seeds
In the dark of my nostrils
cockroaches run to hide
Back of my eyes helium glares

The world is no more than a small rock
soaked with the downpours of raging poisons

the centuries are withering behind us
as if they never existed

I too am a tatter
of burnt human creature
in the afterlife of earth –

beyond the horizon I hear
my lost remains calling to me

galaxies burning at the stake

Great Wave

we saw the world end
in a ball of fire

two balls of fire
& puffs of dust
outrunning gravity
blowing off
the laws of physics

2 planes took out 3 towers
it was a miracle it meant
anything can happen

in reality
it was the Middle Ages
mind-bending demons & wonders
mounting a comeback

the Enlightenment
was shockt it decayed
into too many words
with too little to say

brain waves heart rhythms
emanations of the flesh
mirrors of the soul
warped   that day
their ashen darkness falling away
like the great wave of Hokusai,
the vast horde of its waters
storming up & over
the little fishermen
in their little boats

Mt. Fuji shines
in distance
white & serene

...we woke
to fire & smoke
small bodies on TV
holding hands
walking out of windows

buildings
give up their ghosts
over & over
on TV after TV
spewing toxic dust
haunting down the day
of panicked faces, eyes
running half looking back
at the science fiction
choking their streets . . .

Hokusai's fishermen cling
to the gunnels
of their slender boats

the Great Wave
the menace
& beauty of it
hanging over them

is as perfect & as still
in its blackness & blueness
as Fuji in the brilliance
of its canopy of snow

it is what it is

here nothing is

we have learned to read miracles
as signs of a conspiracy

we manage to live
with murder & torture

in the name of a homeland
we never lived in

trapped in a web
of blood-&-soil,
fear like a filthy sack
pulled down over our heads–

we will never now *not* see
human beings rendered
walking on air, as though
treading the heaviness of water
feeling for the bottom
for all to see
the dignity the immensity
of their death, & of their littleness

against the spectacle
of the New American Century
where the world we knew ended
–floor by screaming floor–
in the first murders of the terror war

Silent World

Gaza: Operation Cast Lead

an evil spirit
in an evil time,
a boogeyman
in a nursery rhyme

schedules them caught
outside the school
going & coming
class to class
all on a Saturday morn, O

all on a Saturday morn

coming & going
when & where
coming & gone
without a clue

& yet this is
no mystery

with nary a word
nary a whirr
bombs rain down
from too high up
for anyone to hear

from too high up
for us
to speak of

not murder, no
we have no word
for murder, but
a blacked out

magic act that
can't be topped –

as they disappeared
betwixt & between
home & school
coming & going
or standing still

you could have heard
a pin drop

Green Hill

on the green slope
of a green hill
picnicking
over Gaza

an epic vista
with binoculars
(all the better
to see it with,
my dear)

to dance & sing
to strew
to slop
happy happy garbage
down the green slope
of a green hill
celebrating the carnage

shameless the joy
that makes an orgy
of others' misery

in Jerusalem later
spitting at Armenian priests

As the UN

overruling
its own rulings
talks itself senseless
bled of sentiment
like an old teddy bear
leaking stuffing

the gods beat on it
with phosphorus
sophistries lies
& worse yet
lame shit

The Year 2008

hardcore drunk like some
obscure Roman emperor
risen from centuries of darkness
smirking, at long last
finding his inner god
the President fumbles for lipstick,
scribbles across the mirror
just, please, try to stop me

only to rub out the *please*

    *

history is being rerun
sort of: an epic production
beautifully choreographed,
including the reviews

the birth of a nation
is reconceived as
the rebirth of a nation

'if we want things to stay
as they are,' says Tancredi,
'things will have to change'

thus, the three towers
flouncing, descending
in ungainly stateliness
like antebellum matrons
spitting tiny figures
out into a netherworld
of red gray dust

the blood & soil
of the New American Century

    *

white house congress courts
central intel media
breathing hard together
simulate conspiracy

in a similar but not
same way waterboarding
simulates drowning

of course it's not really
drowning, not till
strapped to the tipping board
cloth over face
the drownee breathes

*

so it comes to pass that
these wicked children
who are not children
skate on the waters of life
they have not drunk of

it's a bloody miracle,
skating on water

we've learned to dread miracles
because who knows
what they'll savage next?

the only mystery is why
no one has stopped them, yet

*

lord forgive them if they kill
moremoremore fasterfaster

if the kill rate falls off
if they hesitate or leave
the slightest doubt

they could be caught

delivered to the street like Mussolini
          the first *real* fascist
in shirtsleeves, yet humanly naked
with his beautiful mistress Clara
poor Clara, who did not deserve this,
wasn't political, but wrapped in herself
alongside bald Benito
her skirt tied at the knees, their arms dangling
hanged by the heels in a gas station

          *

meanwhile, back at the ranch, the running of the cartoons...

Hillary, Queen of the Jungle
beating like mad the war drums for the big cats
that will eat her up

          *

And Obama! Wingèd Boy King
caught
nesting in the web of palace eunuchs ...

yet don't panic, don't fear
for him this is pure theatre

the fine rolling voice saying all
anyone ever wanted to hear

the smooth fresh face
bold & brilliant, like a poster
pasted over the rotting corpse
of change we can believe in

to keep things as they are

O Bama

o the pathos
of a con man in a con game
made-up under the knife
      face lifted
to look like a republic

already swallowing
the ends of his sentences

Chorus: Greek Marines
at the Siege of Troy

translation: Sophocles, AIAS

When, when will these wandering years
add up to something, anything
to put an end
to this spear-driving backbreaking work
on the plains of Troy
whelmed in the shame and sorrow of the Greeks.

He should have been sucked up into the sky
or plunged into the black hole
of ever open Hades –
the man who taught Greeks
to combine forces with hateful arms
for making war,
exhaustion reviving exhaustion
to kill men.

The thrill of myrtle garland
brimming shallows of wine bowls
sweet crescendos of flutes
all that that man has taken from me,
taken my sleep
and love making love into the night.
I'm left out here, who cares?
my hair sopping wet, sodden with night dew,
never to let me forget
I'm here, in miserable rotten Troy.

Was a time massive Aias held off
nightmares, and waves of arrows.
Now he is given up
to the brute demon that pursued him.
Ahead
what joy can I see?

O to be blown homeward
to the wooded headland towering up
over the beating sea.
To sail! under the high
tableland of Sounion
hailing all praise to blessed Athens

The Gospel According to Saint John

In the Beginning was the Word
& the Word was made Flesh
& dwelt among us

you yourself know
however long or often you've held
your breath, beholding
some archaic torso of Apollo–
from the intolerable silence,
the muscular glow
of the marble rib cage,
must come the word
beyond words
turning, torquing its longing
on you, as Rilke's did on him–
the weathered crotch at the apex
of a barely surviving thigh
propped by an iron bar, there
it is, its broken sex crumbling
like a veteran of the wars, saying
there is no place that does not see you,
you must change your life

yet how change the life that
has and has not changed you?
life that like a Heraklitian fire
you thought you'd gotten through
unscathed – yet see, suddenly

                    you yourself
are the maimed stranger
who scared, and saddens you

because the word incarnate
is also Cavafy, a species of priest
& of a certain tendency, who
having heard too many confessions

turns on you, weary as dusk, saying
much too quietly for comfort:
you say you want to leave here,
go somewhere better –
you will never leave,
as you've ruined your life
in this one little lifetime
you've ruined it
everywhere, for all time

& that is why – in the wheedling words
of Keats's crush
on Fanny, whom he hardly knew –
that is why I write to you – not, like him,
wielding death as a weapon, threatening
to die on her (& following through)
but only to say – as I, like you,
never did learn to say:
this living hand now warm and capable
of earnest grasping
look! I hold it towards you

because the word beyond words,
the agony that never sleeps,
that leaves
incurable wounds,
the beauty of it
piercing through and through
all we thought we knew

is flesh, and dwells among us

Aias in the Morning

up before everyone

before wife,
before son

first up
in the still of the morning

the nightlong blood
he has dragged through the killing fields
slides, dreamlike,
from his sword

the queer thing is
the obscure stuff of life
is obscurer still
in the morning light

he stands in it
like a statue
without a pedestal

he remembers only
the soft slap of the tent flaps
against his arms, going out
in darkness to kill
the arrogant commanders
of the Greek army–

above all to whip
the shit out of Odysseus
for swindling him
out of Achilles' armour . . .

beyond this he remembers
nothing, but waking up
chest and forearms
matted with blood

mind blank

he does not see
how could he see
killing and killing
there was no light to see!
how he salvaged his honor
by savaging the innocence
of sheep, oxen, noble goats,
bewildered herdsmen

as though *they* were
the thieving Greek warlords–

he does not know, yet
the honor he slaughtered for
makes honor itself
despicable–

so Agamemnon lords it still,
Menelaos struts and struts,
they can't stop
lording and strutting . . .

even now
Odysseus tracks him
in the blood muck

where nothing is sacred
no one is saved

Homecoming

he thought he'd come home
free, yet finds himself
at the end of the earth

where it is morning, and still
too early –

when the mist burns off,
when sunlight slips
through the ravaged trees
like a gentle hallelujah

he will recognize nothing,
not a bird, not a leaf

it will be as though
he has crossed the River Styx
into life
as he no longer knows it –

a riot of flowers will be
waiting
waving, wilding their heads at him
like grotesque life forms
demanding to be lopped off

what was dearest
he will feel least for,
what was pastoral
will be most brutal

like a snapping turtle
sticking its long neck
out, to hiss and spit

music will be torture

when he climbs the fence
to walk in green, open
sunny space

his wife, his son
will look up at him
with small, blank stares
like someone else's sheep

White Phosphorus

it looks festive

a geyser
of high arcing foaming-over stuff
dangling
puff balls of ganglia

there is no known human
way to frame this:
the many unsteady
tentacles reaching out raining down
over farms & villages, on every living thing

we could hear their bodies burning

there is no known
image
of dense inert metal explosives

infinitesimal
tungsten, blown
like metaphysics through flesh
melts bone

leg bones of the half girl
losing definition

here the horribly died
three, laid out in a row—
eyeless carcasses
like charred tissue papers

these strange looking
things wrapped in sheets are loved
now, with such a love
it can't tear itself away

no one sleeps
this love off

their strangeness
so creaturely
makes thinking itself strange
& feeling, stranger still –

their tenuous
burnt-to-a-frazzle look
has me thinking
I confess to thinking
what I cannot imagine
of the Amaretti wrappers
we took the sugar cookies out of
& rolled into cylinders
& stood on end, & lit
– just these past holidays –
subdued flame crawling
down, in fascination
burning off the green blue & red
barely legible writings & designs
until, relieved
of the weight of the world
floating their empty blackness up

they settled gently down

here, where the slightest breath
moves them in their stillness

these the belovèd
barely holding their fragile shapes
barely
the sweetness that was in them

Early Poems, 1967-1994

Let fall all the leaves of the earth
Masaccio never painted, and fall
from the sky nothing but rain.

from 'Expulsion from Paradise', by Alejandro Romualdo
(1926-2008)

Facing Up

A croak out of the marsh in the dark hollow,
drowned chord roaming.
It broke into our sleep.

                    Then
this March morning, plopped in the dooryard –
that old familiar amphibian

marooned on the crabgrass (a more rugged green)
unmoving, and bigger than life
being blurted out.

                Unbeautiful
who turned up, perhaps, for air.

...It is the Frog Prince
under a spell of wishing, just under
a cold archaic smile,

having come so far, in mottled skin
green and darker green
like dappled leaf, sick, bewitched,

through shades, through clammy depth
coming to be kissed.

Midsummer

Coventry, Connecticut

That the high sheen of death could blot
this green away, or life survive
the great ice age, is almost not

to be believed. Clearly, today's
raw sunlight ripens into grass
and grazing cows, as though always

it has been so. Still, glacial rock
like giant bone pokes through the earth
and weighs the age-old walls that block

these fields, the livestock locked within.
A herd of motley, white and black,
the cows browse in oblivion,

their muscles ruffling under veils
of gaudy, violet-winged flies
aswarm their hides – and swish their tails,

thickset, but limber as bullwhips
perpetually in motion, long
quick lengths unravelled at the tips,

from side to side. Nearby, a brace
of mules tethered to iron stakes
stand stock-still. And out through space,

at times, too far away to hear,
a flashing Sabre-jet transcends
the mules, the massive cows – a mere

slow-motioned slip of silver light –
and wakes a ghostly rainbow arc
flatly across far hills, its slight

exhaustion burning through the blue
useless sky, trailing away,
its destination out of view.

The glacier's gone. The cows assent
grassward, earmarked with metal tags,
delicacies of ornament

that glint and tick away the sun
as their ears twitch, as they remain
one pulsing mass – as if each one

had undergone the bull, the calf,
the frost-bit rains, and now held out
for nothing less than life itself,

nor cares that space thins out, goes dumb,
that time may cease to come–as if
rockbound, this were the kingdom come

and the hunched fields were crystal-clear
Jerusalem, and life was judged
vibration in the summer air.

I Frammenti

Brela, Dalmacija, 1963. Remembering Stipin Juričić, his family & their hospitality.

1.
Snapshot

Stipin at 74
still poses
paterfamilias stiff
in lavender light

having his picture snapped.
Badly mended
cracked spectacles
gravitate down his nose.

Up the smudged, backsliding folds of road
serpentina, a woman tugs
a big-bladdered goat
wobbling through the dust,

a cascade of pebbles
falling out at the heels ...
Stipin's wife. Untreated
cancer mushrooms in her

voluminous black blouse, under
the mound of dry goods,
no disaster
but the fact of life.

Beyond all that,
buoyant
on homemade wine and pride
the old man will wave good-bye

eking out broken Italian:
Quan ritorn tu
saro nel
Paradiso.

2.
Memento Mori

Coastal hills
volleyed cuckoo echoes.
They backed us up. They
cut us off from the interior.

The covering of pine trees
the fragrancy
died
down along the beach.

Hollow
hoarse
a jackass hee-hawed
airing the dry heaves.

Raked-over shingle
rattled into the Adriatic
quietly clapping its bones.
No matter

what stones we scaled
how flat
how many times
they dropped out of sight.

Even the washed up sea urchin,
a raspberry-speckled egg
shocked with spines
like a contact mine

crumbled
powdering our palms . . .
Islands
flourished offshore

virtual Hesperides,
and the miniature
motor thumping ferry
running out like a series of duds

touched back and forth, and forth,
suddenly snuffed,
so undependable
we could depend on it.

3.
'UN COUP DE DÉS'

Night, night. Stipin
fiddles with short wave radio
tuned in
to news from over the water.

Out for a breath of air
among the pines' antennae
I clear my head. Both
up and down the hillside

the scattered, vaguely whited houses
lodge at a tilt
like chunks off the moon
coming to this,

no village
but a settlement
where the lime-riddled stone roofs
hold up

as if by pure luck
or less,
a throw of highlights
on the heavily wooded rise.

Crew Practice

Lake Bled, Jugoslavia
for son John

I'd wave the gnats away and try
to tell you, *no one is more dear*,
unable to tell, or think why

and justify our life besides,
hardly in touch. As like that shell's
fanning water, our shadow glides

down to the dark bottom, beneath
consideration nearly... Past
the feudal castle, with each breath

striding much like a galley, or
a leggy water bug, men drop
airs, ages lost in the Great War,

the Austro-Hungarian Empire
and pine island astern – where still
an alpine church upholds its spire

but holds it, also, upside down
in the water mirror, as though
gravity dragged images down

and drained them off. So many lives.
Caretakers raking the far shore
burn off a winter of wet leaves,

the column of smoke leans. Swallows
blow over all day, worrying
sunset–like quick, following harrows

until the sky yields. In widening rings
they orbit, then come back as bats
stroking raggedly on damp wings

equipment in perfect order.

Whenever overtaken, I
duck, nor trust anyone's radar,

not even theirs. Then, when I look
at what comes true, or listen, hard
by the flat tension of a lake

while gooseflesh rises, recalling
how the coxswain's regular bark
marked time, forced rising and falling,

or out of habit think on Proust,
how little we know or love, those
we know the best and love the most

then, man to man, this heartless view
tempts me almost to tell a lie
and wish you better than I do.

Blueberries

'The feast is all around us.'
(G.C.)

Up in a clearing of the wood, beyond
the wavering incline behind our house
– wild among scrub and poison ivy –
we find the high bush variety.

Hung in the hot, sticky air
under the leaves,
in two's, and three's, and one's,
each delicate worldly sphere appears
refrigerated, fresh – a full one
dusted with blueish, flat-finish mist.
It picks up fingerprints.
(The gentle brutes rub through, as though
accidentally polishing the genie's lamp.
Patches of deeper blue break out, ragged,
and galaxies glimmer in the distance...)

Juggled, bruised,
piled in the bucket, they burst
with diminutive spiky tufts; they leave
an impression of darkness shiny with use –
a heap of old ball bearings wearing through the grease.

And we have clung like these.
                              Consider.
Off in an otherworld – the end of *this* world
clarified by perspective –
obscure, rotating sentinels
hold smoothly to the dazzling capitals, the columns;
they have turned their shoulders to the wheel
wearing shoulders down. Too soon,
even planets wobble under astronomical laws...
After 29 years of rage
my belly drops into rampant middle age.

Our vulnerability remains, the saving grace.
Lost in an unspectacular cranny,
battered, manhandled,
we are neither false nor true.
O blueberries, whose blood is juice! All together –
who entertain, perhaps, an aftertaste
of the banal, heartfelt, metaphysical abyss
reaching up and cutting through.

Fish in Winter

translation: Joseph Brodsky

Fish live in winter.
Fish nibble oxygen.
Fish swim in winter,
grazing their eyes against
                        ice.

There.
      Where it's deeper.
Where the sea is.

Fish.
      Fish.
            Fish.

Fish swim in winter.
Fish want to swim out.
Fish swim without light,
under a sun orb
              wintry and shaken.

Fish swim away from death.
Ever. That is the way
              of fish.

Fish do not shed tears,
stiffening their heads against
                    bluffs of ice.

      In cold water
      the cold eyes
        of a fish
        freeze

Fish are silent, always.
For they're –
              dumbstruck.

Rimes about fish,
                like fish,
stick in my throat.

A Jewish Graveyard Near Leningrad

translation: Joseph Brodsky

A Jewish graveyard near Leningrad.
A crooked fence of rotting plywood.
Behind the crooked fence they lie, side by side,
lawyers, shopkeepers, musicians, revolutionaries.

For themselves they were singing.
For themselves they were saving up.
For others, they were dying.
But first they paid taxes,
                    deferential to the collector,
and in this world, desperately material,
interpreted the Talmud,
                    remaining idealists.

Maybe they saw... more.
Maybe, they believed blindly.
Yet they taught their children to accept
and to hold out.
And they did not sow the wheat.
                    They never sowed wheat.
Only, they were laying themselves down
in the cold earth, like seeds.
And were falling asleep forever.
And later, earth was being scattered over them
and candles were lighted,
and on the Day of Atonement
hungry old men, their high voices
pinched with the cold, cried out for peace.

And they were finding it.
                    In the breakdown of brute matter.

Nothing, no remembering.
Nothing, no forgetting.
Behind the crooked fence of rotting plywood,
within four kilometres of the trolley turnaround.

Dropping Out

'It is impossible to live in a society and to be free of that society.
(Lenin)

Twenty years ago, witch hunt meant congressional subpoena:
slap with a paper glove. Now it may be a shotgun.

No one's career is ruined anymore,
because career is an obsolete word.

Success is swallowing what's left of pride, the way
others crash on pleasant drugs, intending suicide.

To get up and go to work is pushing genocide
the poor and intelligent say –

although the worst hasn't yet come true
except in principle.

Today, paranoia. Tomorrow, Delmore Schwartz back from the grave, saying
even paranoids have enemies.

Rumours clutter the kitchen table
like bomb threats piling up in public telephones.

The question is not if or whether
but when and how.

In your heart, you've begun to weigh moral distinctions
between one murder and another,

your heart sinks
to the level of a court of law.

Behind you, your childhood is littered with truths
you thought anyone would die for –

like the leaves this fall, the wretched yellowing
of white shirts no one bothers to wear.

No more the blazing, breathless
redgold of a sudden cold snap!

                    Leave?

Wherever a man might step, it seems, he put
his foot down on someone's neck.

Avenue of the Americas

for Grandin Conover (1937-1969)

Back toward Sixth Avenue
    at 3 a.m.... with you
musing, padding along the concrete.
Without
      warning you flash out, disconnected
as a news bulletin:
    'This is it
the most degenerate part of the city.'
                           'Why? What's ...'
    'Because,
it's the Avenue of the Americas.'

In a week I'll phone you
Police will answer, not pigs
but something human
      intoning: 'I'm sorry. I don't know.
I didn't find him.
You must feel
      They just left me
to watch the body.'

Tonight though
you show me
      your seedy haunts.
So they won't be lost

Bars are air-conditioned
caves.
At the International you call attention
      to the walls –
shirtless cowboys, heroically drawn
      steel workers pouring
molten steel.

Socialist Realism? You wonder at
        the proletarian ideal.
The studs-and-leather crowd mixes it up,
bruisers
        huddle, making love.
The way they look, they might have stepped
        off the walls
into this hole
An oldtime communist bar
for workingmen.
You raise the question, 'Is this
        what the 30's have come to?
Or was it, even then
what that scene was all about?'

We slip out.

Some hangout by the docks, we're thrown
back to the 50's.
It's like high school.
        One pool-shooting dude
plays at Viking, hair swept back
        like deep swells at sea,
striking goatee...
He doesn't make it.

Well-built derelicts post
        themselves at corners.
Each with his doorway, storefront, or leans
        one foot cocked back
against an iron picket.
Scouting the sidewalk
        for a pick-up, it's
themselves they ignore!
You can't
        figure them out
'Not even by sleeping with them'
you say

We glide by
          out of reach,
like a tourist with his guide.

At the White Horse having left
Jim and his girl
Agreed she's no less
intelligent than beautiful...

Night before, you'd dreamed
          you married Jackie Onassis
She scrubbed your back in the bathtub
her knees dug at your skin.
          A little man in dark glasses
you kept begging her to let you in...

And we'd
Agreed, too, next time I visit
          to pick up
a couple of Eastside chicks
and spend lots of money...
Camaraderie.

At dinner we'd talked of Vallejo
          and winced
poor bastard,
collecting bottles for his bread.

Later I threatened
'you won't get away with
          'Proposals for a New Society'
I'm writing a reply.'
You laughed
          amused
and, I think, happy.
You could dig that.

...Suddenly I'm in a cab.
You're standing in the avenue
Neon pallor, like a terrible psychedelic poster
          saying something
I don't understand.

You reach in the window to shake hands.
In 10 years we have never, even,
        shaken hands.
Now. I cannot understand.

The cab takes off. You step back
Your last words
sear,
      a parting shot:
'You know I've always adored you.'

'Dig it Grandin' I
      toss back, abstracted
as if I hadn't really heard.
Lighting a cigarette, scared
Trying to brush your words off
      like hot sparks.
My shirt will burn.
My ship

I never bargained for this.

'E. 67th' I tell the cabbie
once more,
rounding a corner.
Speed
     eases me
back into the seat.
I'm fugitive. The window's open
     on all that
dying out behind me, downtown...

You're saying
'You know, I've always adored you.'

                Yes, I know.

To Arlene

In your eyes of Pole and Yankee and Jew
       our homeland bleeds
and the night air –

Pack the bags
button up the children

We'll leave.

I'll love you
as Nike loves the mad rush into nowhere
       headless and wingd –

Over Berkeley: choppers
       lullaby
spraying the campus with gas.

In a Middlefield swamp: icepickt, scalded, shot
a black undercover agent
                or patsy
Where is the line to be drawn

Darling
your thighs are fresher than the broom's
                yellow flowers

To be lost in so many thickets –

Domesticity plunges into poetry
                more dear
with the madness coming over this sad land

and against your cheeks
and through your hair

Walking with Deirdre

That rush you thought was river water –
    it was spring
clearing over the boulders.

                     Once, from underfoot
a ruffed grouse flew up like a terrified heartbeat...

To open a window
 Pasternak observed this
    before he melted into the landscape –
is to open a vein.

Walking with you
            opens a door.
Flushed, it's glorious, what is there more?

I stand here, cold as the mountains
    the March sun begins to warm
and water trickles
           running out of the rock.

Deirdre, bountiful daughter, we'll never die out.

In Cuzco

September 1973

Something they had to celebrate
                    so came
            bundled in ponchos
the sodden colour of old copper,
and in alpaca skullcaps
            with pom poms
with earflaps curling up, ¡ay!
and bare feet, cardboard shoes, in suit jackets
    round-shouldered as the cobblestones,
and high-domed panama hats
                painted white,
white with a black band
                    and in petticoats,
in chemical blue
tennis shoes

a trumpet they had, flutes
beating at skin
            drums and a bass drum too.
and placards waved in the dusk: as though
            swatting at bats
                    with wands
brushing away the Cerro Corporation
            its yanquis, its paper
    deeds
rattling their chains in the dark . . .

Dispossessed of all
but original insolence
                    (the heart in its ribs
            like a bloody flag in a fist)
they quick-stepped
                through the cold wet street,
hupping and fluttering a red flag

American Love

Peru X.73

We did not sacrifice
the human, but had

40 and more
kinds of potatoes,

a few to spread out
on strewn wet grass

these we left: 4, 5 nights
to freeze on the ridge

and each morning, underfoot
squeezed the moisture out

till they were hard as rocks
and kept for years

but soaked in warm
water an hour or more

they softened and swole
they made a stew

and no one starved,
we always had food

we never *had* to say
I love you

Toque De Queda

Santiago de Chile, 1973

Already the greengrocer's on Merced
is shuttered up.
    Who cares
now, if he charged too much,
or that his thumb worked greasy miracles
            with scales

What few people are left
        are newspapers the wind blows
over and over. What difference is it
    what lies they told,
what stories
buried

That one, with the bundle tucked under his arm,
he was a child once
    clutching its pillow,
    His head's
            wrencht
over his shoulder, where the fear is

And the fat man with a limp, it's terrible
to see him hurrying!
He was not built for this
    but for an easy chair, a sweet illegal
pastry: of sugar, flour, butter.
But with a hunger
    now
no black market can satisfy,
he drags and is swinging his leg
    as though it were young, gawky and flighty
            O so wild
as never could get enough out of life

Fascist Pastoral

Santiago de Chile, 1973

What did you expect: blood?
But blood dries up,
      nights
            come home
like a flock of smudged pastoral poems

Are fairy tales what
      the poor wish?
then pastoral is the propaganda
of the sordid

Running lights out
      helicopter hovers
with its rabbit thump, rabbit thump
      And sharp dull
clatter of shots:
      like planks
slapped down on a lumber stack . . .

But muffled, as a held breath
      all night
mushrooms: a slumridden
      meadow
of raw wood shacks.
          Which at dawn
beg to be burnt to the ground.

LISTEN THERE'S BLOOD, BUT BLOOD ISN'T
THE WORST THING ON EARTH
What is, is people suffering their silence
      like sheep –

who had only aspired to suffer
as human beings

The Day of the Night

The day of the night
they arrested Fernando:
I'm lounging on a bench
among retired old men
and purple flowers
in the Plaza de Armas.

A one-legged man
rolls his sleeves up
and hums: over
an iron water bubbler
bubbling over
his hands and forearms.
Having dropped his crutch
he's washing away.
The worn out
blue of his shirt
is gray as the overworked sky.
He could be a cloud
        blue
bird with spindly legs,
standing, one leg
more or less straight,
the other tucked up
under its belly:
tossing a splat of drops
off, onto the packed dirt
under a huge leafy palm
that droops and crests
– but motionless –
in carbon monoxide
it can live with,
the way an oasis
lives with desert.

He will stand
72 hours, without
a thing to eat,
a black
hood over his head.

If we had wings, petals, roots
we wouldn't be human.

Elementary School

Santiago de Chile, October 1973
In memory of Teresa de Jesús: teacher, poet, life force

Why is it the trivial saying
warbles with rage, and fear.

Shaken. *This is the rain*
that kills the little birds.

She said birds, she meant
children.

The rain was weapons
inspecting the books,

the rain was dollars, a hush
scudding across the earth

the rain was workers, peasants, it was misery
raining tears, blood, dirt.

What after all was rain
but the lesson –

that birds were children
the wind blew, the rain struck and slurred . . .

until the children learned
they were not children,

nor rain rain,
birds birds

Isa Mar

for Isabel Margarita Letelier & in memory of Orlando Letelier,
assassinated by a car bomb September 21, 1976 in Washington, DC

1

What a get-together it was
in the New York restaurant.
When your hair tumbled down
        to your hips
Pablo went wild over it.
Baptizing you 'Isa Mar'
        – as a dark sweet-toothed water
                running over –
he scribbled
        you, or her,
fugitive verses on napkins.

You were rushing back, into
        the mercurial black
sea syllables of Isa Mar...

Isabel Margarita stayed on the shore.

2

                        Isabel, what do you hear?
Your husband's marooned: off Tierra del Fuego
        on Isla Dawson.
It's a small world, smaller than the moon
Its tiny fires illumine no one.
                Day and night
                        watchtowers train their sights
into the concentration camp,
others
        stare at the sea.
No flushed human face
swims into view.

But welcome
        penguins
like ambassadors, who keep their distance.
The Antarctic Circle brims with wildlife,
why is it
        it transmits nothing
but waves of cold and wet...

No longer under house arrest,
but doing time
in this plush apartment
            your eyes widen, globular.
Flesh is heavier
because your heart is.
You could be a page boy
            nibbling,
                waiting for messages,
your hair cut and set.

Behind a TV screen
            as in a shadow play
the general gavels his fist.
His captive audience
            is 10 million souls.
His office is so close
The polaroid windows
                    reflect
        a feeble brass sunset
down at your window.
When he opens his mouth
        all Santiago
contracts to a shrunken head

The poet is dead.
                The Ministry of Public Works
lugs his urn from one rented mausoleum
        to another.
His land can't live with it.
Which tosses and turns
        in the General Cemetery
like a relic thrown into the sea...

Isa, in grinding silence
        between one hemisphere and another
the scraps of poems
to you, went under

the soldiers taking Orlando away from you
took Pablo's poem, too

                3

In your purplish dark
        mother-of-pearl look, there's
a cave to curl up in:
                listening
to cold black waters
crashing sidelong at the shore

                        ...out of which comes
                Pablo
fleeing the hospital, the mummy beds
of Santiago.
He needs
        Isla Negra
to die in.
He loves the brute
    semiprecious stones.
        Loves what
bursts into life, like birds!
And wants, and gets, a wall cage of creaks and flutters,
an iridescent tapestry
                that preens, couples, sings, craps,
whose feathers fly.
He wants the bliss
        of dying
where life throbs and is shameless,
because it's the only way to live.
        His bed is set
kitty-corner in the room.
He gazes at the sea
        going from iris to blue to black, to green
and iris, out through the window...

                    Orlando too shows up
as *Fanta*, with his orangey gray hair.
When he called his office, who answered
            but a general.
He held the phone up in the air:
            'Listen
to the voice of a traitor.'
Then ate his breakfast, read the paper,
in utter calm
            is driven to prison.
                              In Dawson
he makes a tin can coffee cup
and well, with a reed-like handle.
            Behind barbed wire
he won't be cowed,
and won't
            stoop to shout.

Your days and nights
            eddy and stream around
this russet rock,
this still standing man.

O but here now
where earth ends, old
General Pinochet
            pokes up
                  his grandfatherly head,
Barking like a seal
out in the mist.
His eyeballs
            sting, he can't
sleep, can't see
through the blood web.
And is addicted
            to stiff white uniforms
like self-torture,
To recall
            how crisp
and clean it used to feel?

What happened to the boy
his mother called
                    Augusto, Augusto!
    What's left
gropes awake in a strange familiar blood

Your black heart heaves and heaves
too deep for hate.
You turn these up
        and slip away, saying
live a beautiful life

                4

Recall, Isabel, the nights
you plunged in icy water
            over your head –
so young, you and your friends
played as porpoises.
But warmed up
on raw pisco.
That was the life then.

And once a Gypsy took your money.
Cursing her you yanked
        her thick braids
off, they were fake!
You were both so shocked
she gave the money back...

Isabel, this is for you,
for the cold,
for the stolen scraps
        of poems to Isa Mar,
for the rest that won't come back
because it went without saying.

It's true: curlicues of praise
        like ribbons
refuse to be wasted.

If Pablo knew anything at all
this is what he knew.

You're not the wrinkling, stone deaf
       body of salt and water –
but a high-spirited, enduring woman.
But a girl, a girl too
who answers to Isabel
       Isabel Margarita!
No poetry is lost on you.

Guerrilla

Santiago de Chile, 1973-74

After so many lovely faces
went ashen, too delicate for words

and skittered away
until their backs looked like backs,

we hunkered down
and sang: horribly, but sang.

And when we swallowed, we brooded,
our skin listened

to its own cells, its buried children
giggling in the dark.

And wept for the inch deep brook
stroking its moss, the swamp

of yellowy woods, sticks with petals,
and the shaggy hump of meadow

glittering with spittlebugs, fizz-drops
brimming their joy to the edge of the wood...

Spit on our lips was beautiful
struggling to say love is what it is.

Facing up, up, we found ourselves
in this sorrowful army, the army that wins

by rage, and error, and by winning over
but always, coming only to be kissed.

Now Sing

NOW sing: the guards howling
beat him with obscenities.
    But he did.
His legend is
He was singing
        Venceremos
when they shot him.
Even for them, it was too much

they killed him,
they couldn't kill him enough.

Victor Jara
     sin guitarra
who'd held out with bloody stumps
                  and sung

Raging Beauty

Having come so far, I find
myself on a street corner
                of North America.
Hair sharked back with water,
blade in pocket,
ready to cut
        anyone's throat
like 20 years ago.

I never left.

Now in the glass domed
Museo de Bellas Artes
I stare
    like a barbarian
at works of art:
                at *Bride of the Wind*,
        at *Caryatid*,
the rarified shit
wishful men and women
        end up with,
Who grope for beauty everywhere
but where they are.

The daybright dome is almost
beautiful as sky.
                It is.
But what does it sing to itself
        at nightfall
alone in the dark with its acre of dusty hall,
its few sculptures
like gelded boulders...

                The river's
spitting distance away. Bridgehead too
        I go to –
where pure hearts have painted
bold graffiti:

verses giving birth
            to hammer and sickle banners,
    Silhouette
heads conceived
            bald as slates, but red
yellow white and blue,
As bright and primary
as a nursery.
            New as it is
                    it mildews,
                            The muddy shallows of the Mapocho
ripple every inch, stopping at nothing

until 20 years have gone by
like a rusty knife...

Until I'd give anything
            to go away
myself, with the river,
Not now, but someday
free to rage:

            'We didn't
diminish what we touched,
we weren't
children forever
but stood ground, and grew,
what we made we made
                    human, with a human face'

standing on this bridge
between the 19th century museum
                and 21st graffiti,
between one death and another
while the horrible water runs under

Song of the Spirit

translation: Quechua song

      Spirit, little grandfather,
little old man with the face of a rat,
the tip of the nose moth-eaten,
the backbone a long saddle sore,
the mouth spouting drivel,
the palm begging to be greased,
the left eye always running,
the right ear broken off,
little foxy with its tail tangled up,
vicious little runt of an ass –

that's you as you are, Spirit,
little old man with the face of a rat.

What are These

translation: Quechua song

What are these?
They're senators! that for
a mingy salary
will start a war.

Mariano Baptista
the great speechmaker
I stick on the rooftops:
that tightfisted milker.

Mendizabalcito
has plunged into the mud
ah! but he's gotten up
all covered with gold.

Look at that
senator, look inside him:
nothing! No, but
his pockets are stuffed.

The priest of Mizque
has written me, saying:
'Senators!? You might as well
cut off their balls.'

Mendizabalcito
has fallen into the water, ah
but he's gotten out again
dry as a bone.

Senators of the valley
can't find their tongue,
because they don't have one
they cultivate their fingernails.

   Every mother's son
lives on his land, in his house.
Only I, poor exile
have no home no homeland.

   What Jiménez de Asúa said
is clearer than pure water:
'Among our presidents, is where
the biggest thief will be.'

What Cloud is that Cloud

translation: Quechua song

What cloud is that cloud
gathered so close?
Probably my mother's tears
turning to rain.

I'm a man travelling alone,
I have no mother no father,
until even the tree by the road
is a tree that gives no shade.

Bringing me into the world
my mother said: 'You will be a man.'
And father: 'You'll be a worker
and a slave,' he said. And wept.

Between this day and the next
I leave on a long journey.
If there's life, I can come back.
If death, not ever again.

Purely by chance, I have a mother
that I may have a father
that he may say, some day:
'Where is my son?'

Beauty Parlour

translation: Alejandro Romualdo, Peru

Gold
and misery
of Peru. Parlour
of horrors
and beauty. I have said,
seen
and heard, with my soul
clinging to the earth. I see –
being born in blood, the face
of the rose, in night the day, in afternoon a sky
wide open as the carcass of a steer, the gold
pure under the sky of gold.
I see
the sun
being born, the day
dying, daily, in flames,
and this is the same – or almost the same –
as a graveyard of living rot.
And the sea
goes on, the sea rolling round
like a hoop in the sea, the sky
face down, I go on seeing
and hearing
drenched children in the streets, begging
bread
they pay only thank-you for, good-bye for
the misery received.
Everything
muttered, all
disjointed, lying there, broken,
I see
misery coated with smiles, meals
eaten off newspaper, and I hear
the sun from a silent bell
sounding out

against me, against everyone,
for having pointed the poem into the ulcer
the parlour
(of beauty and horror) in which we endure.

Angel in Flames

USA, late 1970s

Angel on this broken street
is dressed to the teeth.

He has his dignity.

*

Under the dove gray fedora
there's a wage slave
out of work.

He has his dignity
against a wall.

*

And under
the wasp-waisted shirt,
extravaganza of black volcanic glass
crusht in daisies
ay! there's the merest rib cage,
bird bones of winter,
a sallow angel

*

And in the
quick brown eyes
like worry beads
that cannot read,

and the fingers
with their walking stick
which is really a weapon
that cannot write –

there is the bonfire of poetry

*

Angel is a slave out of work.

Someday he's going to kill someone.

*

His small hands
have flown at clouds,
sick with blood
with glass
banks shimmering in distance,
the sharp
stink of weed,
stone throat,
star
sapphire
flash and rush of cops...

*

Graffiti
choke the street,
blaring off these walls...

*

Angel in flames
will blacken the sky

Frankie Reyes' Poem

Willimantic, CT

is missing.

Because what's missing
here,
and not only here,
is Frankie's first lesson

(after 32 years put off
he's nervous as a cat,
            but
the woman sits him down
with A, B, C, etc.
worrying to bits
a gnawing
sleepless
rat)

because without him
between these lines,
as between the lines
of bilingual
signs in emergency rooms,

here
is a terrible wound

            *

Because where are
all, or just one of
his sentimental letters, soul notes,
his pages of roses and moons,
of 'treasure'

where, his playful
machismo
not to be condoned, and yet
where is the gala he is,
the
party wherever he goes

because without this
labels on soup cans
are ghastly, tin, stripped
of the simmer and whiff
of cream of asparagus,
of chicken noodle

*

(where is it
the first, unrehearsed
note to his tutor,
a tart
    'X is a brat'
to tease her, but
also to pay her off,
what she has given him
letters for)

*

because with this
poems may be poems
not crippled
    precisions,
and leaflets to his life
might not be
bossy, puny
    slaps in the face
but speak, eye to eye,
not glazed
not aside

*

Because what's the use
if we can't

                    (coming
home from work at 1 a.m.
that
night after the first lesson,
scratching away downstairs

at 3 a.m.
wake Sharon up
                'Read this read this'
so beside himself
how can she get mad?
                        'Huh?'
handing her a scrap of paper
'Read this, what
            does it
                say?'

        as she mumbles, mumbling
        it
        in a daze...

and with
Frankie pound the bed
'I thought so!
I thought so!
I thought that's what it said!'

slamming the walls of the
universe back

like a boy his huge
intelligence
beaming, all
over)

        *

because without this without
him
every line,
but especially these,
skips a beat
as it sinks into
something like night

because without him

there is a quibble in the heart
of your joy
and at the heart of your rage
a melodrama

a lie

Down Home Prison Poem

for Luis

We come as friends
with the best intentions

to commiserate,
cheer you up, discuss
lawyers, cases

bandy about
Frankie's latest, confirming
who drinks too much
who seasoned the turtle stew
how good it was,
how Ralph still
talks about a job
as though he really looked

and what guys hang out
still, on the stoop,
catcalling girls
on Main street

or who skipped town
on charges
to be lost
in New York, New Jersey, Miami

slipping like fish
into a sea of Spanish

we come to go
over this

like shadows come
to tell you
without telling you

in so many words
and yet, without lies

the great world, the
life is passing you by

you gone gray long before
they locked you up, to look
at the floor now, seeming
so far away
saying under your breath
so none but us will hear

I've seen things here
in all my life
I never thought to see

Esperanza

The bony black face
of Esperanza

archaic face
of blood work, chicken
slaughter, pinfeathers, salted carcasses,
of hands condemned to glow
in cold dreamless water,
cold cement
stopping the feet dead

the look of work
and strike, one more
picket with a slag foot rhythm
that says, we won't kill ourselves,
we can walk this line forever,
or what amounts to forever...

Esperanza is sick of forever.

On the strict iron
of the fire escape, she bristles
like chilblains in sunlight
resting her bones against the warm brick wall.

Against the world, which is
legal and Anglo, she yanks
a lavender vinyl collar across her face.
Not like an ostrich, but an old opera.
They want her soul her bread
her food stamps, welfare
check, slave pay,
her 30 dollar a week
union dole.
Her man, her coat.
Even at night
she pulls the night over her head.

Even her cunning
gets carried away
on the wings of her innocence.

The cold damp air
is killing her.
She's picking up what she can,
flying back
to Puerto Rico,
wherever it is –

a thin black bird
good morning'd and fed,
have a pleasant trip
as never before, never again,
in the belly lap
of a huge silver bird...

coming down into
factory clouds of sunset chemicals,
flecks of ash,
the queasy
blue wrinkled bay water,
skimming and overshooting
rows of stunted
pineapples withering in the field

a few shreds
of fading colour,
the same earth
she had come from, gone to, and left.

A swollen super port
rose from the sea, draining the sea.

Limousines
sped past vacant lots, gardenias

a mountain of nickel,

gouged face...

Esperanza
shivered to bone
in the throats of restaurants,
in plump bodega hearts,
and in the labyrinth of refineries
– high flying
            torches
                        burning off the night –
in the sublime
filaments of computers
that could not swallow her,
and cannot spit her out.

Now all the hand-slapped guitars
put on
smiles of glass.
They have a mouthful
of sharp dark bird, petty
thievery, acrid
envy

Esperanza
fills their mouths with blood.

...Unborn skies
come to stare: at broken
palm fronds, broken words,
at what seem to be
hands
wrung like flags of shame.

To stare, and wonder how so much
wealth made so much poverty
so much alone,
how so much misery
made Esperanza
who expected
nothing

scavenge in the cracks
of her own hands only

to bury her face in the dust of Puerto Pobre.

Enough!

for Hazel and Poppy

And now they are no longer
man and father,
woman and mother,
but 2
workers in old age.

Her, she's
a tiny cell of light
– 40 watts, say,
against three backyards
and one small, dirty side street –
in an immense night.

She dreams no more
than the dog, Toro,
chained to the back porch.

Six days she goes
out in the marbled mist
of street lamps, dawn, dripping trees,
the sky
with its wisp of moon.

Sundays she sleeps.

Across the city, by the harbour,
the cable coiling
machines she tends
are not what they are
but the oily roar
of her horizon.
An end.

And him?
Back from the hospital
he sits in the kitchen.

His brain scatters
wishes
and insights, like fireflies
through the terrible spring night

only to say
how dark it is,

how 38 years
boxing chemicals and beakers,
grinding glass,
add up
to $57.60 a month
for life: enough
for dog food, cheap
stupefying wine,
rest beyond belief.

It is more
than enough.

With Awful Luck

translation: Aztec, c. 1521/28

With awful luck, pained we saw our pain.

      Broken lances
              lie in the roads,
hairs are scattered about.
The houses are roofless,
their walls hot
      red hot.
Worms sprout through the streets and plazas,
the walls are flecked with brains.
Waters are red, red as if dyed,
and if we drank
      it was saltpetred water.
TERRIFIED WE BEAT AT THE MUD WALLS
and we were left with our heritage:
      a net of holes.
We put our lives behind our shields,
but shields do not hold off
      the desolation.
We have eaten crumbs of bird seed,
we have chewed bitter dog grass,
adobe chips, small lizards, mice
and ground up earth and even worms...

Workers United

WILL NEVER BE DEFEATED
OBREROS
UNIDOS
JAMÁS SERÁN VENCIDOS

A militant
unarmed march
to the Brooklyn Navy Yard.

Usual signs,
banners.
Usual chants
wave after wave the same

Suddenly
held up: at
the tinkle of glass.
Distant, tiny, shocking
like the death of a toy

Frosted panes
broken
a fist emerged, a forearm
a face, another...
In gloom 5 stories deep
a hand started
waving
from the bottom
of its life,
as a sea fan
rust streaming
ships have passed over

Now
short thick leggy
fingers
hook through the window grates:

undocumented workers, illegal
aliens
from South America
Africa
the Caribbean:
shouting
French, Spanish,
tilted and musical English,

the human rainbow
arrested,
detained.

It had been Bolivian
with Indian cheekbones

It had saved, waited
to cross the Rio Grande
packed in vans
and car trunks
to be shot at,
raped
in the moonless dust

It was Haitians
on rafts
pushing out to sea

landing in these
marine gray
block buildings,
crosshatch fences
coiled with razor wire,

and around these
a field of black
Brooklyn ghetto,

a prison
in a vast
crumbling prison,

becoming this
protest
against this.

Above all it would be
the voice
from a broken window, trailing
down at the end
thonk yoo
thonk yoo

it blew a hole
through everything

In the Decadence of Eternity

May 31st, 1978.
Our dwarf star
lolls, still,
over the parked cars, the glass
and chrome, the tar,
the worn naked railroad tracks.

Here, where we live,
workers
are driven into the earth
like spikes. Not gold
but iron,
rust.

They link
age to age,
landscape to landscape,
clay pits
to the brick backs of towns.

And now
the 2 o'clock
train rattles and squeaks
over parched cinders,
easing into the freight yard.

A crew of gandy dancers
in magenta hardhats,
some in undershirts,
some with kerchiefs,
lay down their tools.

They step back
in burning puffs of air
to rest,
it is their right
to rest,
still as shepherds
while the grinding wheels pass.

Cold Rags

Where did everyone go?

Enemies depress the air.
Friends have gone home.
What's left
is comrades.

If only *these* were not so
remote, righteous, intimate
as gossip in snow.

If they would stop
lying to themselves.
Or if the lies
warmed, were not
wrinkled
and stiff
flapping at the skin.

In such comrades
a comrade could freeze to death,

to death
pushing this brilliant future,
this communism, this human
truth
like a needle that has lost its thread.

Winter Journal

That winter
outside the Palazzo Farnese
the fountain froze.

I'd sat alone in the Sistine Chapel
as in an old barn

So bone creeping cold
even the guards had gone.

Against the Judgment wall Michelangelo crumpled
his own skin like a trophy

Adam, waking, had already dreamed the God
rather than face himself...

What went wrong? that we'd got up to make
a masterwork of our misery.

The sky, if it had feeling, would also grow old
wrote Chairman Mao.

The guards, they guarded a stove in the storage room
thawing their fingers and toes.

Revolutionary Poetic

You go
dragging the poem with you.

It doesn't want to.
Has excuses, reasons.
But confused.

How will it squeeze
through, with its
hands in its pockets?
How continue
cultivating tears, airing kisses?
How can it with justice
howl, without
its luminous rage
that never got angry,
that hardly ever
hurt anyone?

And where will it put
the children,
their dew darkened trees,
the pleasant
threat of rain?
How keep
unbroken, unspilt,
the simple glass of water?
Which is. Just is.

And old old innocence
that took
the stick, the cold machinery,
responding only
with morning

with warm steaming milk?
How give *that* up?

Surely it's easier
for a rich man to enter heaven
than for a poem
to step sinking into revolution –
like Moses
marching into the desert,
making for his promised land.

The poem facing its future
feels like Moses,
the rich man.
When it goes, it can't
even
take itself.

What, then, if it's stuck
paying dues,
magic marking slogans, saying
'this is how it is, and how
it will be'
and thinking
second thoughts.
Revising, to say,
'actually, *this* is how it is.'

What if it goes on
saying and thinking
and is not perfect?

And how, when it goes,
can it keep
kindly, or cynically,
superior?
What if it kills someone?

Worse, what if it doesn't
and is, instead, itself
shredded and pulped?

And if it ends in the dump
with other cadavers
also mutilated,
also scarred,
until even the scars
are stripped from its bones..?
And if, at this landfill
of black plastic bags,
gulls are still
dipping and cresting
over
like a gale of papers,
and swallows
or whatever they are
are darting into the sand banks..?

Then you just, must,
tell it the truth:
that, well, that's life
and how it goes.
Take it or leave it.

When you go
don't expect to come out
smelling like a rose.

Halfway

1

Halfway into Paradise
               Dante hears
the advice he wants to hear:
'Tell the whole truth.
No lies.
If it stabs them
        sick, even to tears
let them pick at their own scabs.'

That's what I say.

I say that.

2

Now I hear
        a pure spirit or wise guy
put this burning question to Chou En-lai:
Why. Why didn't he
        push the revolution to the hilt
and finish the job.
Chou replied, 'Look here
        look at my mother.
She has bound feet.
What can she do
        but hobble around.
If I cut them loose, she would fall down.'

That's what I say.

I say that.

3

So torn the gut

          howls in its pit

Witness César Vallejo

We call on
comrade compañero
César Vallejo.

We assemble his
corrections
passions
exasperations,
his nimbus
of humble respects.

To his card carrying
communism we appeal,
his blank passport
utopian
forehead,
his vest and shoes,
his marxist-leninist study groups.
And, why not, his arrogance
his fractured earnestness
so literal!
and the blushing
aureole on his pillar of militant light...
Why not!

For his palm pledges
the muscle pump
crammed into his chest.
For, in fact, 40 years dead
the corpse, which is very dead, is yet
very warm –
like a book face up
under a single staring lamp!

It has taken dictation,
it translates
oxygen in blood.
But whose, where to? What says
this same comrade
compañero, for whom
the correct line was a spinal column
not a rope or a stick,
for whom the precise path followed
in footsteps
of the Spanish workers' militia
and through a maze
of International Brigades carrying
their countries on their backs –
what does he say? this scribe
whose future was as the reptile
left behind, observing
the shoulderly, the modest, the anguished, the firm
pass it by...

Who meanwhile gritted teeth
at the wretched, shouted
'Get up!'

And with one nail scribbled
'Do not lie'
and with a painstaking thumb
impressed on everyone:
'Trust the workers. Speak with your
production, how much
human you produce,
or shut up.'

Who having exhausted
this last vein of irony,
breaks off one last
message after the last

saying, simply,
'Serve the sovereign workers.'

At which he begins to sweat bullets
bridges
clouds
& this and that
& with his navel
his stunned Peruvian clay
his Parisian rain
he sits down, cannot go on.

He has forgotten himself.

Now
there is no César Vallejo.

Where César Vallejo was is
the abrupt
erect
million, 100 million, 800 million
souls of workers,
each knowing something
it alone can know,
some angry, some embarrassed,
most plain with wonder
but none, not one, is cold

before this witness
whose passion is our verdict

Golden Mean

They call the rage of the oppressed
extremist.

Evenhanded
censure,
from the hypothetical centre of

the slaughter they call impartial, objective

North End

Hartford, Connecticut
16 years old, two children, struggling alone

Peaches, I tell it cold as I can.
Let the explainers explain away.

That winter's morning after class
you stared out the window into the filthy wind
        the honey-coloured slum
and said, as though saying nothing,

'when I wake up in the morning
I don't want to wake up'

Pathetic Fallacy

And yet a camera is more
human than a penguin

this doter will ponder
weeks months in rows
the one white egg
balanced
on its broad feet

but the telephone hung up
on a desk
cord dangling
is more
moral immoral

the black and white
bundle
staggers off into spring
unable to fly, flops

tipsy and formal
into a groaning smoking sea,
plunged into

sub-feeling cold
in which
it has no need of us

is this amusing, moving

and yet
a machine a Volkswagen
beetle

a diesel rabbit whose
grandsire may have
been a gas chamber

is more human

Poetic Diction

Certain words are not fit
for poetry.

Boss, for instance.
Our better verse
you may observe
has no boss in it.

The best, in fact
the most refined
has eliminated jobs
strikes & lock-outs

not to mention unemployment.

Naturally there are no classes.
Rather, no ruling
and no working.
Just, on occasion, a middle
or an English.

It follows there is
no exploitation
no struggle
no poverty
no racist taunts
or murders, and
no injustice

because there is no
justice –

only psychology
begging questions, and

trees, menstrual blood (it's
OK it's animal nature)
with a few obscenities
classical compositions
dewy or sweaty
love, but not often

mystery, fantasy, myth
an insane asylum,
victims without victimizers
as in slabs of veal,
and a little peace

there is peace
in poetry, the
pie in the sky
of this vocabulary

which you can bet your bottom
dollar does not include
the resilience of the
less than poetic people
nor their intelligence
seeing right through
the culture police.

This is why no one
minds
poetry anymore –

its world is one
nobody lives in, not even
poets who close their eyes
to speak

Poe Votes

Wednesday Oct. 3rd, 1849
all liquored up
and dragged
(Crane guesses)
retching through Baltimore
polling place to polling place
to Ryan's 4th Ward,
each time a different
dead man, with
his semblance of a life,
and each time
under another name
this same sad man
dying those deaths
became
a whole gang of votes:
this sorry man
jingle man
this haunting
genius of American letters

'When The Time Comes'

When the time comes
I will do
what must be done

he said, and meant it

even as he spoke
the time had come

What are we Waiting for

after Chile

We are waiting for the moment
to make our move

as we did in
fact, in the capital city
under dusty palm trees, wait out
splintered bursts of gunfire,
the body of naked rags
bunched-up at a snag in the river

yet this too passed

oranges tumbled into market bins
all by themselves
the children took a bus crosstown to school
someone disappeared
we had another cup of coffee
3 days later we heard
he had been picked up about the time
the kids were coming home from school

what could we have waited for
a solar eclipse? declaration of war?
what was so unusual?
it was just another day

now gone. You eat
an apple, work out, have
a glass of beer, water the cactus
once in awhile
read a book, vow
to be honest and straightforward
hedging only a little

cheating only
on death, taxes, beauty and, sometimes,
the harder truths

but in how many days
who will tell you
nothing was as it seemed, say
who has been taken away
or maybe a job
possibly yours, or
everyone's social security

and that the world we see
we live in
does not (never did) exist

Winning the Moral Battle

losing the bloody war
the honourable few

advocate passive resistance,
go limp –

the bodies are dragged off
like dead bodies

They Glorify Non-Violence

because the violence is directed
against someone else

because they think the violence is directed
against someone else

because they do not see
how this touches on them

because they do see and are afraid
to call the violence violence

because they can live with it

because they think
they can live with it

because if they name it
they will have to deal with it

because if they name it and don't
do something about it
they will see themselves dismembered

their principles in one room
(at church home school)
their ass in another

because this is how they live,

and if they miss the contradiction
they may watch it on television

pacifists will sit down
under the mantra of non-violence

because it took violence against
others to make their living for them

took strangers subduing
milking and mining strangers

to refine them, to introduce
legacy offspring into Harvard

it took yet more violence
graphic and distant

a massacre or two on which
to exercise their fine moral anguish
on what, to them, is exotic

it's a relief, they feel
at home with it

because this is civilization
as they define it

Poverty is a Bloodbath

therefore we oppose poverty
as we oppose bloodbaths

we are against violence
it solves nothing

we are against poverty
it is hell on earth

against violence we advocate
non-violence
the antidote to poverty
it's obvious, is money

for the mutual problems
of violence and poverty
this is *right honey*
the solution

a non-violent philosophy
with property and money

Poor. Paradise.

Coming at last
into our own land
we were
where we are

Alone together in another slum
bristling
          like cactus glory in the desert,
We too
          erect were bliss
We wished only for what is.
My heart was in your mouth
Blood under your skin was juice
          easing my lips
Our word came forth naked
courting what is.
What is
          blessed us, blessing enough for us

One human being was no human being.

In our tribe everyone starved
or no one did

Fist & Letter

translation: Alejandro Romualdo

Put
the letter
in your fist: Write, write, write
against wind and tide, against shadow,
against this whole horrible masquerade
that passes daily before our eyes.

Put
your fist
in the letter: And blot, blot, blot out
the blood buckling us in, the shadow
spilled across the soul, the terrifying
misery
that peoples the face of charity.
Strike
with the letter.

Put
your mouth
at the bottom
of this pit: And sing sing, sing
truths you can put in your fist.

If

capitalism kills

it's not always with a bullet
into a black,
not always a radiated worker
high on grass, packing
an old atomic sub reactor
in concrete, for burial at sea,
not always in boxes of boys
stiff as marines

it kills

naturally, its
murders
are suicides, accidents or justifiable
homicides, most don't appear to happen,
even if you aren't laid off for life
cut off
how can you make ends meet
the flat jammed who wouldn't scream
at husband wife kids
one kid yelling down the street
I'm gonna bust that fuckin spic
the girl shy to the point
of torment, scratching at dirt
a third fakes karate
grooves
superhuman concentration

who wouldn't

blow brains out
to alcohol drugs soap operas TV football
music music music motorcycles
quick lays
stereo on the porch, out the window, in boom rattle
rip offs betrayals whiplash comebacks *screw you*

not that there are not
good times too

the car up on cinderblocks
months on end
working it over with a beer
in the slow close sun of a Saturday afternoon

though no one in the beginning
chose to live this way

no one wanted

to crash racing around
and around, just to get on,
to not to be
rust, used up, over
whelmed by this system
whatever it is
this gelatinous mass murder
this amber where
they are more and more stuck
turning more colourful, sporting
more flagrant heraldic tattoos,
Christ's head on his bicep, the blue
butterfly alighting at her shoulder,
this turmoil where they are
moving yet still
in colourful clothes, colourful language, ever more colourful
freedoms that don't fly,
deaths that hardly ever
got out alive

from this atrocity
where the man beats the woman
breaking glass in the night

this agony, where they are beautiful
yet hurtful to look on
like a live wire, broken crackling & dancing
dangerous in the street
going nowhere

Capital Punishment

the parents of the dead girl
hang around the prison

they have one question
did he express remorse

she was eight years old
too young for sex
never mind mutilation

did he express remorse

no, no, he went to the chair
'without making a statement'

but did he show remorse

the parents of the dead girl
demand remorse
but quietly

all he ever said was
he did not remember
like nothing had happened

exactly, exactly
that is why
they haunt this prison
its cold stone

they too are children of a sort
they do not want this death

what do they want then

they want
the abomination
of natural justice

the tears of things
blood gushing from the stone

Rhododendron

for Arlene

You said, there's a poem in that rhododendron.
I said, not for me.
Elizabeth Bishop, maybe, but she's dead:
tough-minded lady with her cigarette
always smoking, I liked her, we both did,
though she did make that racist, sexist
remark about cigar rollers in Tampa.
The words out of her mouth left her
propped at the podium, like a quaint
raspy doll... the air
had left the room, left her
standing all by her lonesome,
like a period piece.

Which wasn't fair. It wasn't *her* there
but her in a sea of faces, grasping
for anything not to drown in it,
forgetting how she'd got here: how
the flat sceptical voice that kept
damping down the pollen dust
kept stirring it up, praising it
with the rapt attention of attention
blossoming into poetry – and how
with a few colourful exceptions
she hardly ever got carried away
or lost touch
with the bug-eyed, detailed, luminous rush
where time broke off

where there was a poem
in the rhododendron

*

But what I meant was not
what Brecht meant, either, asking
what times are these when
talking about trees is almost a crime,
because such talk is so much silence
about so much horror.

How could it be criminal
to speak of trees!

I meant: the horror, or what
that cloud of a word covers up,
has come over
the look in the rhododendron,
has left only
this fleshy leaved bush
of big beautiful flowers

but where's the poetry in that?
where is Elizabeth?

                    *

(what I remember is
the bright snappy day,
genoa sails popping out
fantastic blues, oranges, reds, slippery greens
leaning and skipping like berserk bloomers

we were flying a kite out over
the shallow scallop waters off Duxbury
hauling, tugging
before the line broke

though the kite was so far away
by then, when the twine
dragging like cable, parted, surprised

we didn't mind, in a way
we were relieved, giddy

Elizabeth fluttered a little
and was, clearly, pleased

*

one day we're caught looking

bumblebees and brass-jacketed flies
poke about heaps
of milk pink fluff

as though the yard were 13 or 14 years old
again, beside itself with its first
floppy corsage

the rhododendron grew so fast!

blossom to blossom
blew, crushed

we're puzzling now the odd
petal in each cluster,
the yellowish thumb smudge
of darker, yellower spots

we are watching the sun
grow quietly old

*

trees have something to tell us
we could not tell ourselves

*

Ar, I do thrill to some poems
I mean, the honest that open up
looking right at us,
opening us up,
I enjoy the rhododendrons

the pink more than the purple,
they're so fresh
they will never be accomplices,
it's not that I can't feel for this
or for Elizabeth, or what
made Brecht cold as leather,
doesn't it get to most of us?

but if there's a poem is this
it will have to be
you, saying
(don't ever stop saying it)
there's a poem in the rhododendron

(insist, insist) there's a
poem in it!

What is Poetry

We know it doesn't rhyme much anymore
but is it beautiful is it true
does it transcend the moment
which moment

or is it ironic, does it echo, echo what
does it have ears

at night whom does it adore
yet at dawn
what dream would it go to the wall for

or is it vituperative, why not
doesn't it express powerful feeling,
an overflow of feeling, is it sincere
is that enough

does it lay bare the soul
or explore the give-and-take of intense personal
            interrelationships
which persons, what kinds of interrelationships
work or play or
why one and not the others

is it witty, profound, wittily profound, profoundly witty,
is it avant-garde does it shock the petty bourgeoisie
who love it

or is it above the social arena does it circle the earth,
            a satellite with a proper sense of gravity high
            above the winds of fashion
who put it up there
does it transmit breathtaking pictures of a tiny earth
to a tiny earth

if not, is it a vision of eternity
tell us about it

does it make anything happen
or does it die to itself, till others notice the smell
is it shrill does its voice crack
or must it be a baritone of honey

does it give pleasure, does it teach, delight, uplift
whom does it persuade
whom doesn't it

is it a set of rules a code of forms
what is the principle behind the rules
was it handed down and by whom
or pieced together in a workshop too long ago to remember
can it be rearranged on the shelf
who really cares
may it be dismantled

is it moving, either way moving
is it the imitation of an action
which action

is it a bunch of willy-nilly impressions
who is impressed

if it were a crib
would you trust your baby to sleep in it
bounce up and down in it
learn to stand up in it then
don't answer that

is it a world created by the poet
for the poet of the poet
does it exist for its own sake,
but if it's a way of breathing, whose way
do they smoke are they
breathing making love or getting off work

is it the ideology of a class or the puff of genius
genius for what what class
what are you talking about

is it a man speaking to men
a woman speaking to women
or universal human speaking
to no one in particular
that is, no one at all

is it a mirror held up to nature,
to human nature,
or is it an escape, is it
a mirror held up to nature, to escape human nature, or
a mirror held up to human nature
to escape human history

are you afraid of it
do you understand it

does it embody human values,
values as they are
or as they say they are,
which humans, which values
is it for or against
or does it take no position,
where did it go then
does it levitate, is it in heaven

is it then beyond all this
what is it, where, if you know tell us

but if you don't know
shut up, we'll understand

NOTES

Listening to Coltrane is interleaved with a quote from Coltrane, who was very clear about what he was doing. He did not aestheticize, nor settle into cruise control formalities or stylistics. The depth and scope of his vision was such that, as a fellow musician remarked, 'He didn't want to be out in front like a lone genius. He wanted to bring everyone with him.'

There is No Truth to the Rumour When, on Constitutional grounds, White House aides objected to renewal of certain provisions of the Patriot Act, President Bush responded: 'Stop throwing the Constitution in my face! It's just a goddamned piece of paper.'

Boxcars 'What are boxcars?' The question arose at a meeting of oral historians. Perhaps most participants were too young, or too removed from railroad yards, to have experienced a world in which boxcars loomed not only in reality but in imagination. But then no one under the age of 65 has experienced the Holocaust, either. It is known only in mediated forms, through books, family stories, TV and cinema histories – some documentary, but most fictionalized as 'entertainment.' Now, having achieved mythic status, the Holocaust is less a historical event than an instrument for exerting political, economic and 'moral' leverage. It is used to justify Israeli policies and to demonize enemies of the West, who are routinely cast as 'Hitlers.' Even so, our mediated experiences of the Holocaust have changed over the past 6 or 7 decades. From late in WWII up through the mid 1960s the Holocaust, or Shoah as it was called, served as the quintessential *humanizing* event. It was something that must never happen again. Not to anyone. Yet during that same period the Holocaust narrative was being appropriated to justify the military and civilian occupation of Palestine via ethnic cleansing, apartheid-like legalisms, and flat out crimes against humanity. Those of us who were ignorant of actual post-Holocaust history, who took Zionist mystification and self-mythification at face value (I recall the general exultation at the Israeli victory in the 1967 June War) found ourselves trapped inside a juggernaut that in time would become 'part & parcel' of the reigning orthodoxy of U.S. political, media and cultural institutions. 'Boxcars' is then an attempt to recover the intensely mediated process whereby an understanding that was entered into in good faith found itself hustled into a tribal mode, ultimately a militarized ideology, that is in principle and practice antithetical to the concept of humanity.

Dadalab 'High from the Heavens I Come' is a Christmas carol verse on John Heartfield and Rudolf Schlicter's satiric mobile, *Prussian Archangel.* Hugo Ball and Emmy Hennings were seminal to Dada. Marcel Janko, like Tristan Tzara, was from Romania. The Dadalab is in the Dada Museum that Janko founded at Ein Hod, 20 km south of Haifa. (The museum website claims he founded the village as well!) Dadalab is advertised as 'an interactive exhibition in which everybody can assume the role of a Dada artist, break the bounds of conventional art and engage in interdisciplinary creation. In the Dadalab everything is possible…'

Strange Words Jean Améry (October 31, 1912 – October 17, 1978), born Hanns Chaim Mayer in Austria, was active in organized resistance to the Nazi occupation of Belgium. He survived internments in Auschwitz and Buchenwald and was liberated from Bergen-Belsen in 1945. Among other works he wrote *At the Mind's Limits: Contemplations by a Survivor on Auschwitz and Its Realities.* Améry committed suicide in 1978. The incident recounted here is not from Améry, however, but post-Saddam Iraq. The incident described here is not from Améry, however, but the account of a man 'renditioned' by the CIA.

Qana Thought by some to be the biblical Cana. Modern Qana is the site of two 'sleep-killing' massacres. The first occurred in 1996, when Israeli artillery killed 106 refugees sleeping in a UN compound. Ten years later, on 30 July 2006, the Israelis bombed a basement shelter where Lebanese citizens were sleeping. Of the 56 people killed, 34 were children. The bomb, a laser-controlled BSU 37/B 'bunker buster' with a depleted uranium (DU) warhead was supplied by the US. Years earlier, in a similar instance in Gaza, IAF General Dan Halutz was asked under judicial inquiry how he felt bombing a tenement. His response: 'What do I feel when I drop a bomb? A slight bump in the airplane.' During the 2006 attack on Lebanon the Israeli military complained that the Hezbollah-led Lebanese resistance camouflaged their rocket launchers with moveable trees. They kept firing and moving, before the IDF could pinpoint their locations. Coincidentally the flag of Lebanon features a cedar tree.

Atahualpa Death Prayer is based on Odi González's recent Spanish version of 'Apu Inka Atawallpaman,' an anonymous Quechua poem that resonates with the epochal fallout of Pizarro's murder of Atahualpa in 1533. No one knows when the poem was composed, but an early date is likely. With one possible exception due to a faulty transcription, the original Quechua has no Spanish borrowings. This is a rare document of the indigenous peoples' own response to the character, emotional impact, and the catastrophic depth and scale of the Spanish Conquest. I'm grateful to Carlos Suarez for helping me through a few difficult patches of the Spanish text.

7 They are 7 Cantata composed by Prokofiev in 1917, the year of the Russian Revolution, when Czar Nicholas was overthrown. For reasons historical and technical (the work is only seven minutes long but requires full male and female choirs, a huge orchestra and a tenor who can cope with vocal extremes) it was not performed until 1924, in Paris, under the direction of Serge Koussevitzky. The 'wedge-shaped writings' are cuneiform, which dates back some 5,500 years.

Anthology of Rapture is a bricolage drawn from a number of poems, chief among them: 'The Myth of Hiroshima' by Saga Nebuyuki, 'Cocoon' by Ishigaki Rin, 'Revelations' by Kihara Koichi and 'The Vision' by Toge Sankichi. All are associated with 'naked language' poetry (*hadaka no gengo*). My own interpolations – including images from *HIROSHIMA-NAGASAKI: A Pictorial Record of the Atomic destruction* (1978), and from a former neighbour who as a Sea Bee (the logo Sea Bee = CB = Construction Battalion) at the end of WWII operated a bulldozer in Nagasaki – are part of this mix.

The descriptions of those who were at or around Hiroshima or Nagasaki are uncannily evocative, but in a disabused, reality based way, of the 'end-time' anticipated by Christian fundamentalists looking forward to the moment when they'll be gathered together to meet Christ in air: '...and the dead in Christ shall rise first: Then we which are alive and remain shall be caught up together with them in the clouds, to meet the Lord in the air' (1 Thessalonians 4:15-17)

Great Wave '2 planes took out three towers / it was a miracle . . .' On 9/11 WTC7 was the third tower to collapse, at the speed of gravity, into its own footprint. It had not been hit by any plane. Its collapse was miraculous. As there is no scientific explanation for this unprecedented phenomenon, WTC7 was disappeared from the final report by the official 9/11 Commission.

The Year 2008 Transition year from the Bush to the Obama regime, a continuum signaled by Israel's *Operation Cast Lead* in Gaza (beginning December 27, 2008 and ending January 18, 2009, two days before President Obama's inauguration). D. W. Griffith's landmark film *Birth of a Nation* (1915), an attack on Reconstruction, presented benign images of antebellum slavery and the post-Civil War Ku Klux Klan. The 'rebirth of a nation': i.e. 9 /11, anticipated by PNAC neocons (one of whom edited the final draft of the 9/11 Commission Report) who had speculated that 'a new Pearl Harbor' was needed to inaugurate 'The New American Century.' Tancredi Falconeri is the consummate revanchist opportunist in Giuseppe Lampedusa's novel, *The Leopard*. The 'red gray dust' is the bilateral red/gray chips (nano-thermite residue) in the dust of the extinct WTC.

Aias in the Morning and **Homecoming** sketch alternative scenarios for the post-rampage dawning – the horrifying self-realization – of Sophocles' *Aias (Ajax)*. In the play, believing he's been cheated of the dead Achilles' armour, Aias sets out to murder Odysseus and the two Greek commanders: Agamemnon and Menelaos. But deluded by Athena he ends up torturing and murdering the livestock that are the Greek army's unsorted war spoil. The poems were written in response to the current use of *AIAS* as a vehicle for dealing with the Post Traumatic Stress Disorder (PTSD) suffered by increasing numbers of soldiers still in, or coming home from, the proliferating US/NATO wars they were or are engaged in.

White Phosphorous The effects of white phosphorus are well-known. It bores burning into the body. As long as there's oxygen to subsist on, it can't be extinguished. However more exotic, 'undeclared' experimental weapons were also used in Gaza, e.g. dense inert metal explosives (DIME weapons, developed by the US Air Force) which are based on nano-technlogy. They leave no mark on the skin, no wound, yet destroy internal organs and melt bone. These weapons are genotoxic, as they also attack DNA.

Avenue of the Americas Grandin Conover, from whom some of us learned so much about the deeper, darker American realities – obscured in the heady 60's, but now fully exposed – was a playwright (*As The Hawk Sees It*, 1962 and *The Party On Greenwich Avenue*, 1967) and poet (*Ten Years*, published posthumously in 1972).

With Awful Luck Source: Spanish translation from a 1528 mss. *La Literatura de los Aztecas*, Ángel M. Garibay K. (Editorial Joaquin Mortiz, 1964, 1970).

Song of the Sprit, What are These, What Cloud is that Cloud Source: Spanish translation in *Poesia Popular Quechua*, Jesús Lara (Editorial Canata, La Paz-Cochabamba, 1956). Jesús Lara, who as a child was beaten for speaking Quechua, became a scholar and made a dictionary of Quechua. He wrote the life and death of Inti Peredo, the complete edition of which was burned by the government in the main square of La Paz. Inti Peredo (1937-1969), Lara's son-in-law, was a member of Che Guevara's band.

Also by James Scully

Poetry

The Marches (Holt, Rinehart & Winston, 1967)
Avenue of the Americas (University of Massachusetts Press, 1971)
Santiago Poems (Curbstone Press, 1975)
Scrap Book (Zeising Brothers, 1977)
May Day (Minnesota Review Press, 1980)
Apollo Helmet (Curbstone Press, 1983)
Raging Beauty (Azul Editions, 1994)
Words Without Music (San Francisco, 2004)
Donatello's Version (Curbstone Press, 2007)
Oceania (Azul Editions, 2008)

Translations

with Maria A. Proser *Quechua Peoples Poetry* (Curbstone Press, 1977)
with Maria A. Proser and Arlene Scully, *Teresa de Jesús: De Repente/All of A Sudden* (Curbstone Press, 1979)
Roque Dalton, Poetry and Militancy in Latin America, (Curbstone Press, 1981)
with C. John Herrington, *Aeschylus: Prometheus Bound* (OUP, 1989)
with Robert Bagg, *The Complete Plays of Sophocles* (Harper Perennial, 2011)

Critical Essays and Reportage

Line Break: Poetry as Social Practice (Bay Press, 1988)
Vagabond Flags: Serbia & Kosovo (Azul Editions, 2009)